Regarding the Tra.

Jimmy Chen concentrated on BS and History at the London School of Economics and Political, graduating in 2015 with First Class Honours.

In 2017 he moved on from the University of Cambridge with a MPhil in Modern European History. His exposition 'Music as a statement of Russian positive energy during the later Napoleonic Wars (1812-15)' was granted the Members' History Prize for the best MPhil thesis submitted through the University of Cambridge History Faculty during the scholarly year 2016-17.

He fills in as an essential correspondences specialist in London and has recently worked in Moscow for a monetary interchanges firm. He has recently distributed an interpretation of General Mikhail Barclay de Tolly's record of the 1812 mission and has secretly composed a few books on Russian and US history.

Enquiries might be addressed to: jschen1812@gmail.com

Editorial notes

Note on literal interpretation: There is no widespread norm for spelling out from Cyrillic to the Latin letter set. I have done everything I can to guarantee that literal interpretations of names and spot names are pretty much as predictable as could be expected. Except for ruling rulers, I give the transcribed Russian names of people even where there are identical English names. In this manner, Mikhail Kutuzov rather than Michael Kutuzov, and Pyotr Bagration rather than Peter Bagration, however Tsar Alexander I rather than Tsar Aleksandr I.

Note on areas: I have endeavored to distinguish the areas referenced in the first text as well as could be expected, giving current names of towns and urban communities where applicable.

Note on dates: Before 1918, the Russian Empire utilized the Julian or Old Style

Calendar. All dates in this book are in the Julian Calendar except if in any case expressed. The Julian Calendar was 12 days behind the New Style Gregorian Calendar throughout the span of the nineteenth century.

Ivan Fyodorovich Paskevich (George Dawe, 1823), State Hermitage Museum, St Petersburg, Russia

Biographical Essay

Ivan Fyodorovich Paskevich (1782-1856) was one of the most enriched officials throughout the entire existence of the Imperial Russian Army. Throughout the span of a long and renowned military vocation from 1800 to 1856, Paskevich rose to the position of Field Marshal and held the titles of Count of Yerevan and Serene Prince of Warsaw. He is one of seven Russian field marshals to be portrayed in the Field Marshals' Hall of the Winter Palace.

The apex of Paskevich's profession harmonized with the rule of Nicholas I (1825-55). He was a nearby friend of the Tsar, fourteen years Paskevich's lesser, who alluded to him as 'Father-Commander.' Nicholas' rule started with the concealment of the Decembrist Uprising, where a gathering of youthful hopeful officials exhibited in St Petersburg's Senate Square for political change. Paskevich served on the court which denounced the Decembrist chiefs – a considerable lot of whom served close by him in the Napoleonic Wars – to death or exile. The concealment of the Decembrists set everything up for the new Tsar's rule. Nicholas was the exemplification of Russia's totalitarian government and his moderate interventionist international strategy acquired him the epithet 'the gendarme of Europe.'

s the most noteworthy positioning Russia military official for a large part of the Nicholaevan period, Paskevich encapsulated Nicholas' imperious and battle ready system. He took an interest in a merciless ethnic conflict in the Caucasus in the last part of the 1820s prior to smothering the Polish Uprising of 1830 – 31 and filling in as Viceroy. His time in office was joined by Russian endeavors to restrict Polish independence and was depicted by the Poles as 'the Paskevich Night.' In 1849, Paskevich told the Russian armed force to smother the Hungarian Revolution against the Habsburg monarchy.

Paskevich's nearby relationship with Nicholas makes him a questionable figure among Russian antiquarians. Allies of Russian patriotism view him as an incredible military pioneer who won brilliant triumphs for the Tsar and the Russian Fatherland. According to the enslaved countries and among Russian dissidents, he addressed the most exceedingly awful of magnificent Russian militarism. Western history specialists have ascribed his various titles and enhancements to his cozy relationship with the Tsar rather than military talent.

Yet Paskevich's prior profession was undeniably less questionable. Charged as a Guards official at 18 years old in 1800, Paskevich was perceived as a capable official and immediately rose through the positions. In 1812 he was elevated to the position of significant general at 30 years old and put in charge of the 26th Infantry Division. As a feature of Prince Bagration's Second Army,
askevich's men were in the cutting edge at a progression of significant commitment, including Smolensk and Borodino, experiencing weighty misfortunes all the while. In this large number of commitment, Paskevich exhibited fortitude and strategic mindfulness. Before the year's over Paskevich took order of VII Corps. He kept on presenting with unique excellence in the 1813-15 missions on unfamiliar soil and was elevated to lieutenant general.

askevich was not by any means the only individual from Tsar Nicholas' circle to go through the change from youthful military legend to implementer of a dictatorial regime.
Alexander von Benckendorff is most popular to history as the top of the Third Section of His Imperial Majesty's Chancellery – Nicholas' famous mystery police. However in 1812 he had been among the officials telling 'flying separations' which assaulted the back of Napoleon's Grande Armée close by the laborers who waged war against the invaders.

The accompanying pages present a concise blueprint of Paskevich's profession, which saw him have an influence in pretty much every tactical clash including Russia during the principal half of the nineteenth century. There follows a conversation about his diaries, interpreted interestingly into English, which cover the start of the 1812 mission against Napoleon until the climactic but hesitant Battle of Borodino.

Ivan Fyodorovich Paskevich was brought into the world on nineteenth May [O.S. eighth May] 1782 to a Ukrainian Cossack family in the town of Poltava, where Peter the Great had prevailed upon a popular triumph Charles XII of Sweden right around a century sooner in 1709. His precursors were among the elderly folks of the Ukrainian Cossacks, and in 1793 Paskevich was shipped off the Corps de Pages in St Petersburg, as was normal for respectable kids in the Russian Empire. Upon graduation in 1800, he joined the first class Preobrazhensky Life Guard Regiment and was relegated to the staff of Tsar Paul I (1796-1801), starting a tactical vocation that would endure the greater part a century.

Paul was removed and killed in March 1801 in a castle upset and was prevailed by his child Alexander I. In 1805 Alexander went with his

armed forces on crusade against Napoleon in focal Europe. Paskevich was on the staff of General Ivan Mikhelson (1740-1807) on Russia's western boundaries, however Mikhelson's unforeseen neglected to show up on schedule to take part in the mission, which finished with the loss of Russia and her Austrian partners at the Battle of Austerlitz.

With the flare-up of threats against the Ottoman Empire in 1806, Paskevich went with Mikhelson to the Turkish front, where he saw activity interestingly. He stayed on crusade against the Ottomans until 1810, by which time he had been elevated to significant general and won a few adornments. In 1809 Paskevich got to know Prince Pyotr Bagration (1765-1812), who filled in as president on the Turkish front from July 1809 to March 1810. Paskevich would later serve under Bagration in the 1812 campaign.

In December 1810, with the experts in St Petersburg expecting the resumption of threats with Napoleon, Paskevich was named top of the new Orel Infantry Regiment which was at this point to be framed. Throughout the span of 1811, Paskevich worked to select and prepare individuals for the regiment. The Orel Regiment was one of four regiments in the 26th Infantry Division, and
Paskevich was named leader of this Division in January 1812.

The 26th Infantry Division was one of two divisions in VII Corps, directed by General Nikolay Nikolayevich Raevsky (1771-1829). The VII Corps was essential for General Bagration's Second Army, positioned in current Belarus. Paskevich's experience of the 1812 mission, where he saw activity at the Battles of Saltanovka, Smolensk, and Borodino are recorded in his diaries introduced beneath. At Borodino his division experienced substantial misfortunes and after the fight Paskevich busied himself with changing his 26th Division. At the top of the changed yet not yet original capacity 26th Division, Paskevich partook in the Battle of Maloyaroslavets which constrained Napoleon to retreat.

In the colder time of year of 1812 the Russian powers crossed the boundary into Prussia and proceeded with their mission. During 1813 Paskevich was entrusted with barring the Polish fort of Modlin. In November 1813 Paskevich separated himself at the Battle of Leipzig and was compensated with advancement to the position of lieutenant general. From January the accompanying year

he was set at the top of the second Grenadier Division and drove them into Paris toward the finish of March as the Austrian-Prussian-Russian alliance constrained Napoleon to surrender interestingly. After Napoleon's break from Elba in 1815, Paskevich was important for a 150,000 man Russian armed force which walked west to go up against Napoleon, yet when the Russian powers showed up in France Napoleon had effectively been crushed by the British and Prussian militaries at Waterloo.

From 1817 to 1818 Paskevich went with Grand Duke Mikhail Pavlovich (1798-1849), the Tsar's most youthful sibling, on traversed Russia and the European mainland. The way that Paskevich was depended with this mission shows his cozy relationship with the majestic family. In 1825 Paskevich was elevated to aide general and put in charge of I Corps at Mitau [Jelgava, Latvia], where in December 1825 he got fresh insight about Tsar Alexander's demise. Following the Decembrist Uprising, Paskevich got back to St Petersburg and was assigned by Tsar Nicholas I to serve on the exceptional court which condemned the agitators to no end or exile in Siberia.

In the late spring of 1826, following a Persian intrusion of the Caucasus, Paskevich was named leader of the Russian powers in the Caucasus. However Paskevich was subjected to General Aleksey Ermolov, the Tsar doubted Ermolov and accepted Paskevich would be more dependable. The conflicts among the two administrators brought about Ermolov's excusal in 1827. Paskevich drove the Russian armed forces to a progression of triumphs which brought about the marking of the corrective Treaty of Turkmanchay in 1828.

Nicholas properly granted him the title of Count of Yerevan. The next year Paskevich constrained the Ottoman Empire to sign the Treaty of Adrianopole. These tactical triumphs won Paskevich a field marshal's implement and he consequently filled in as Governor of the Caucasus.

In 1831 Paskevich was shipped off Warsaw to order the Russian powers against the Polish Uprising of 1830-31. The past commandant Field Marshal Hans Karl von Diebitsch (Ivan Dibich) had gotten an incredible triumph over the renegades at the Battle of Ostrołęka in May 1831 however capitulated to cholera before long. Paskevich drove the Russian powers to progress at the

Battle of Warsaw, stopping the uprising. Paskevich was granted the title of Serene Prince of Warsaw and in 1832 was named Viceroy of Poland. He sought after a Russification strategy which met with significant opposition

among the Polish populace. He endure two endeavors on his life by Polish nationalists.

In 1849 Paskevich got back to the front line at 67 years old to assume responsibility for the Russian armed force which Nicholas I had shipped off smother the Hungarian Uprising against the Habsburg government. In August Paskevich's powers effectively crushed the renegades and he got back to his authoritative post in Warsaw. In 1850, upon fifty years of administration in the Imperial Russian Army, Paskevich was granted another uncommonly made field marshal's stick by Tsar Nicholas, and was additionally made a field marshal by the King of Prussia and the Emperor of Austria.

In February 1854, toward the start of what might turn into the Crimean War, Paskevich indeed took to the field at the top of the Russian armed forces in the Balkans. In May 1854 he was genuinely injured by a mounted guns shell and was subsequently conceded consent to pass on the military to reestablish his wellbeing, at first at his domain in Gomel and later at Warsaw. In spite of the fact that he kept on completing his authoritative obligations, his wellbeing proceeded to decrease and deteriorated following fresh insight about Tsar Nicholas I's passing in March 1855. On first February [O.S. twentieth January] 1856, Field Marshal Prince Ivan Fyodorovich Paskevich passed on at 73 years old in Warsaw.

Paskevich's memoirs

Paskevich left behind memories and diaries covering the period 1806-15 from his association in the Russo-Turkish War (1806-12) up to the furthest limit of the Napoleonic Wars. Being a senior political and military figure until the finish of his life, it is improbable that Paskevich expected his diaries for distribution inside his lifetime.

The Russian message of Paskevich's "Notes of the 1812 Campaign" introduced in this volume was first distributed in full as a component of an assortment "The Year 1812 in the memories of peers" (1812 god v vospominaniyakh sovremennikov) altered by A.G. Tartakovsky in 1985.

Preceding this, main two concentrates had been distributed. The text in this release depends on two original copies held in the Russian State History Archives. The vast majority of the text relates to the later original copy except for two entries which are just found in the before version.

The conditions behind the organization of the journals are indistinct. In light of Tartakovsky's investigation of the paper on which the diaries are composed, two draft duplicates were delivered by 1833-34. Somewhere in the range of 1837 and 1838, after Paskevich sent a few concentrates of his notes to Aleksandr Mikhailovsky-Danilevsky, the authority student of history of the 1812 mission, a significant part of the message was concluded. The last form probably dates to 1852 when Paskevich completed work on the original copy of his memories of the Russo-Turkish War.

The "Notes of the 1812 Campaign" cover the period from the arrangement of the Orel Infantry Regiment in December 1810 up until the finish of the Battle of Borodino in September 1812. There are further fragmentary notes composed under Paskevich's transcription held in the chronicles which cover the period up to the furthest limit of the Napoleonic Wars. It is clear that such notes were utilized to educate the arrangement regarding the last original copy prior to being obliterated. For reasons unknown, no endeavor was made to change these sections into a clean formalized composition. These parts of Paskevich's oral memories were utilized widely in Prince Aleksandr Petrovich Shcherbatov's seven volume life story of Paskevich, distributed somewhere in the range of 1888 and 1904.

Paskevich's memories give an interesting understanding into the 1812 mission, particularly the Second Army's retreat to Smolensk. Paskevich was the most senior official in the Second Army to leave behind a record of the mission. He gives striking portrayals of the commitment he took part in and features the shaky circumstance of the Second Army, which got away from obliteration through a mix of grit, gifted authority, and a lot of luck.

Moreover, Paskevich's 26th Infantry Division assumed a vital part at both Smolensk and Borodino. Paskevich and his men were at the forefront in the two commitment. As a leader on the bleeding edge in the most significant guarded positions which were the objective of supported adversary attack, Paskevich's record completely exhibits the degree of the demise and obliteration endured by the two sides during the 1812 mission. The 26th Division experienced considerable misfortunes in the two fights, and it is demonstration of Paskevich's authority and grit that his men had the option to hang on for such a long time against supported adversary attacks without breaking in disorder.

All diaries are practices in self-defense to a more noteworthy or lesser degree and

Paskevich's memories of the 1812 mission are the same. There is no question that the youthful Paskevich was a skilled general who utilized his drive in the forefront and tested the choices of his senior commanders.
Nevertheless, the way that Paskevich started to direct his memories twenty years afterward and that he was at that point a vital military and political figure by the 1830s may have made Paskevich exaggerate his own endeavours.

Like numerous Russian wellsprings of the 1812 mission, Paskevich's tends to swell the quantities of French setbacks while understanding the degree of Russian misfortunes to exhibit the predominance of the Russian armed force. For instance, Paskevich claims that Napoleon had 170-190,000 men at Borodino while the Russians had 130,000. He asserts that Napoleon experienced 60,000 setbacks while the Russians lost 45,000 men killed and wounded.
The most dependable appraisals demonstrate that the two militaries were equitably coordinated at 130,000 men each, while Russian misfortunes surpassed those on the French.

This isn't to say that the Russian troopers in 1812 were not staggeringly courageous and talented enough to keep control and discipline during the long and laborious retreat to Moscow. Paskevich's applause for Prince Bagration's helpful administration of the Second Army is in no way, shape or form lost, while his portrayals of Platov's Cossacks and their inclination to surprise the foe is very much authenticated in different sources. The Grande Armée was alarmed off guard assaults during their retreat from Moscow, yet the Cossacks had effectively settled this standing during the French advance.

It merits pausing for a minute to feature Paskevich's depictions of the Poles. There were upwards of 100,000 Polish warriors in Napoleon's intrusion power, representing a fifth of the men Napoleon drove across the Russian outskirts. When Paskevich started chipping away at these diaries, he was at that point filling in as Viceroy of Poland with the title of Serene Prince of Warsaw subsequent to pounding the Polish uprising. Maybe spurred by a subliminal hostility against Polish officers, in his record Paskevich depicts the Polish cavalrymen as irresponsible and inclined to being outsmarted by predominant Russian commandants. This is regardless of the way that along with the Italians, the Poles were frequently the best unfamiliar soldiers in Napoleon's service.

Paskevich's diaries have up until recently just been converted into English in the

type of brief concentrates. I trust that the interpretation of the full message I present in this volume will fill in as a valuable hotspot for western researchers of the Napoleonic Wars who are less acquainted with Russian sources. Easygoing perusers keen on military history of the Napoleonic time frame ought to likewise observe Paskevich's record an enrapturing read.

Jimmy Chen

London, October 2019

Notes of the 1812 Campaign

From the start of the mission until the gathering of the two armed forces in Smolensk

Preparations for war, the formation of new regiments, including the Orel [Orlovsky] Infantry Regiment

By 1810 conflict with France was at that point not too far off and arrangements were made for the resumption of threats. The military was relied upon to select fifteen new regiments. In December 1810 I was requested to summon an infantry regiment called the Orel.[1] In January 1811 I was delegated officer of the regiment. From the earliest starting point this interaction introduced staggering

hardships. The overall arrangements for war were with the end goal that restricted assets were accessible for the development of new regiments. I was obliged to shape the regiment from four post contingents, wherein practically the troopers in general and officials had been released from the field for terrible conduct. We got just three majors and a few officials from different regiments. Notwithstanding this we were sent 20 youthful officials from the corps of the respectability, who barely realized how to peruse and write.

With these assets we needed to rush to prepare the regiment, since war was unavoidable. There was no discipline in the regiment. Men started to abandon because of the offense and bungle of the officials. In just the main month up to 70 men left. I was obliged to send close to a large portion of the officials back to the post. I deplored my destiny that while there were such mind blowing regiments in the military, I was left with the most noticeably terrible restrained of the parcel at the very time when we were getting ready for battle against the unfortunate Emperor of the French. I was then in Dokhturov's Corps, in Raevsky's Division and the leader of a unit made out of the Orel and Nizhny Novgorod [Nizhegorodsky] Regiments. The detachment was quartered in Kiev. I demanded to pull out my regiment from the city since it was difficult to maintain

the necessary order, and moved 60 versts[2] away. Three months of intensive training and six weeks in camp allowed me to bring the Orel Regiment to such a condition that it was already the third regiment in the Division. But this success came at a great cost. As a result of my labours and anxieties, I fell ill with a serious favour, came close to death and rested for three months.

The Second Western Army
In October 1811 the Second Western Army was shaped and General Prince Bagration was delegated its Commander-in-Chief. Dokhturov's Corps was relegated to the First Army. Simultaneously the VII Infantry Corps of General Raevsky was shaped and was remembered for the Second Army. In the colder time of year of 1811, I was as yet accountable for the Orel Regiment. I set exceptional consideration on the officials. The fundamental errand was to show them the standards of military discipline. This schooling didn't make them learned men (this, regardless, was totally pointless). I pushed to them that most importantly, what was required in war was fortitude, boldness, and boldness. In 1812 I was

appointed commander of the 26th Infantry Division,[3] though many generals were senior in rank. In Kiev I was honoured by the visit of the new Commander-in-Chief Prince Bagration, who knew me from the campaign of 1809.[4] I was almost delirious from fever, but his appearance improved my health. The Commander-in-Chief flattered me and treated me not as a subordinate however as an equal.

oving to the border

In February 1812 the Second Army drew nearer to the line. This walk through the most incredibly dreadful mud of the late-winter made the soldiers experience the ill effects of scurvy. Of the 1,200 men in the regiment, up to 400 turned out to be sick. In April and May around 150 men died. In each regiment there were 700-800 men staying in the ranks.

The Second Army was then comprised of VII Infantry Corps, that is the 26th and twelfth Divisions; of the Combined Grenadier Division under Count Vorontsov, the second Grenadier, fifteenth and eighteenth Divisions under General Prince Shcherbatov and two rangers divisions. By and large this represented up to 45,000 men. Toward the start of May we got the request to withdraw the fifteenth and eighteenth Infantry Divisions and some save units to frame the Third Western Army under General Tormasov. Instead of Shcherbatov's divisions the Second Army was left with General Dokhturov's Corps, and the Army was requested to move to Bialystok. In May the Commander-in-Chief reviewed the 26th Division, and the Orel Regiment was at that point second. The Army crossed the Pinsk bogs and stopped toward the finish of May. General base camp was at first situated in Pruzhany. The central command of VII Corps was in the town of Novy Dvor, and those of the 26th Division on the boundary of Bialystok province.

Campaign plans

At this time Emperor Alexander, who was in Vilnius at the overall central command of the First Western Army, met a gathering of battle, at which the plans of the ensuing effort were examined. The conflict with France had been for quite some time expected, and there was a great deal of contemplated procedure. Back in 1811 Prince Bagration recommended crossing into Poland before the adversary could assemble his powers. He trusted that by overcoming him in parts, there would consistently be an ideal opportunity to withdraw to an assigned position. This invasion couldn't be done utilizing an enormous power, yet a little separation could be encircled and demolished by the foe, and it was hard to withdraw 300 versts from a mathematically predominant adversary in an unfamiliar land without saves. It was similarly also that this daring arrangement which was hard to execute because of the conditions was not taken on. In 1812, upon the finish of harmony with Turkey, Admiral Chichagov recommended dispatching a redirection in Italy with the soldiers in Moldavia and Wallachia. At first these thoughts were embraced, and accordingly his soldiers didn't sign up on schedule with the principle powers on the western line. Accordingly, two months were lost.

Meanwhile as ahead of schedule as three years already, since the past crusades demonstrated that it was hard to oppose Napoleon in fight, a choice was taken on account of rout or retreat to set up a braced camp. The settlement of Drissa on the Dvina was picked for this reason. The current fortification of Dinaburg [Daugavpils, Latvia], filling in as the right flank, would cover the camp. Be that as it may, the fortification was not finished on schedule. The area picked for the camp was itself unacceptable both because of key contemplations, in light of the fact that the camp didn't ensure the heartland of Russia however just its northern piece, just as strategic reasons, since near the camp there were statures which stretched out along the whole fortresses and even into the back. Another significant burden was that the plunge to the waterway was steep to the point that a military which had to withdraw would experience incredible challenges pulling out behind the stream. Notwithstanding this the right bank of the Dvina River, where every one of the provisions were kept, were not invigorated at all. I was informed that it was not important to encircle yourself with fortresses from all sides, as though doing as such would keep you from escaping them. In any case, one could encircle oneself with channels, possessing them while essential, and afterward there would be no hindrance to get out from the dark field. In the event that the adversary were to cross the stream looking to strike at the back of the camp and the choice was taken to hold it, then, at that point, the fortresses could come into utilization, since then we could

access the provisions. Assuming that it was not the goal to hold fast now, why construct a fortress on the left bank on the opposite side of the Dvina, with a troublesome and steep intersection, while the adversary could generally cross the stream elsewhere.

Fortified camps frequently serve to secure realms, yet such a camp would all the more regularly be the reason for their total ruin. A military crushed on the field without being obliterated consistently stays the core of a future armed force. Yet, with the catch of the invigorated camp the military would totally die, all its best soldiers and its foundations would be chopped down, so it would not leave behind the littlest establishment for a future armed force. Subsequently, the state would lose all expectation along with the camp and the military. The camp at Drissa was picked so that it didn't protect anything, however one could lose everything with it.

hus, in Vilnius, the committee of war chose not to cross the line and not to start the conflict. "Allow God to begin the conflict," Emperor Alexander wrote in his request about the revelation of war. Seeing that the foe was gathering a huge piece of his power between Kovno [Kaunas, Lithuania] and Grodno, the two militaries were to be united to give each other shared help and to meet the foe with unrivaled numbers at the focuses where he needed to get through. To achieve this the base camp of Second Army were moved and the soldiers sent further toward the north. VI Corps was sent among Oishishki and Vasilishki. The rest of the Second Army, securing its passed on flank to Pruzhany, the right took up its situation at the town of Mosta close to Grodno. The principle central command was situated in Vilkovisk [Vawkavysk, Belarus]. Pastor of War Barclay de Tolly kept in touch with Prince Bagration on first June that our side ought not give the smallest appearance to threats; on account of assault to react with equipped obstruction, yet to stay away from fights with the more remarkable adversary, withdrawing from predominant numbers first and foremost behind the Shchara, to Novogrudok [Navahrudak, Belarus] behind the Niemen, and afterward (as indicated by additional directions) either straight through Minsk to Borisov, or to one side of the Niemen to join together if vital the two armed forces or portions of them. Ruler Bagration was requested to keep up with correspondences with Tormasov's Army at Lutsk, with Ertel's Corps at Mozyr, with General Platov's Corps at Grodno, and with the First Army in Vilnius. Ruler Bagration then, at that point, answered (report dated sixth June No. 283):

1. "That the situation of our militaries is too expanded, that ought to the enemy

2.

3.

try to assault one of them energetically, there would be no an ideal opportunity for it to get fortifications from the other."

4. "That our powers are excessively near the line to effectively focus assuming the adversary shows up at a solitary point with overpowering forces."

5. "That once our high level posts set up that the foe armed force is moving toward the boundary, it would without question walk at twofold speed and in case it doesn't find us in our present positions, it would rush to forestall our intersection before we find the necessary resources to convey it out." After this (twelfth June No. 310) Prince Bagration kept in touch with the Minister of War that "assuming the foe were to attack our lines through Grodno and Bialystok, then, at that point, the division of the VI Corps (which moved from Vasilishki to Lida) from the excess two corps and a deficient

number of rangers, which was possessing a space of in excess of 100 versts, he [Bagration] would not possess the ability to obstruct the foe's arrangements on Grodno and Bialystok without removing interchanges with General Dokhturov's Corps nor without giving the foe the chance to go into our region on the right flank of the Third Army at Vlodava and Brest."

In a similar report he said that as he would like to think, "the foe's benefit lies in the way that to separate our powers... that the nearer our military gets to the ocean, the more noteworthy its danger being cut off and crushed. It follows to presume that the grouping of foe powers among Grodno and Kovno isn't anything other than the longing to divert our powers from the objectives of his genuine intentions."

His remarks were left replied, maybe because of absence of time. In the overall central command of the First Army, as time passes they anticipated news about the foe's intersection of the Niemen among Kovno and Merech and settled on another arrangement: General Platov was requested to focus his corps around Grodno and move against the adversary's flank.

The Second Army was to continue afterward, securing the back of Platov's Corps. In case the First Army couldn't take on a triumphant conflict at Vilnius, then, at that point, it was expected that I and VI Corps would consolidate, concentrate around Sventsyany, where maybe (Barclay de Tolly composed), the foe would give fight. Ruler Bagration saw that by following the arrangement to accumulate the First Army at Vilnius with a unit of the Second Army, he would be

set "in incredible peril, so that through the foe's speedy walk to Vilnius, he would in addition to the fact that cut be off from the First Army, yet additionally from his picked way of retreat. That a solitary look at the guide would show that upon the retreat of the First Army to Sventsyany, the foe, having caught Vilnius, would forestall the retreat of the Second Army to Minsk and by taking the most brief way would arrive sooner than he could withdraw there."

These perceptions, taken from true records, shown how well Prince Bagration comprehended the situation of our militaries, and would fill in as a reaction to the individuals who right up 'til today guarantee that he was just a vanguard general.

Indeed, the situation of our military from Vilnius to the Pinsk swamps was just great until when the adversary assembled their powers. However at that point we ought to have effectively expected the results of the retreat and not delay until the adversary's intersection of the line. Assuming Napoleon were just to make a diversionary assault at Kovno to keep the First Army, and were himself to hit at the middle with three corps, that is with 120,000 men, at Grodno and Bialystok, then, at that point, he would just experience Dokhturov's VI Corps with 20,000 men and Prince Bagration's Second Army of 40,000 men, 60,000 taking all things together. He would overcome and drive them away before our soldiers could withdraw from Vilnius. Fourteen days of lateness nearly prompted the destruction of the army.

The resulting occasions fill in as proof of the legitimacy of these suppositions. Albeit the foe entered Vilnius in extraordinary power, they halted there and afterward just sent Davout's Corps to Minsk, yet even with this late development Dokhturov kept away from the foe by a wonder. Dorokhov and Platov had to withdraw to the Second Army, and just with unusual moves, which just Russian officers were fit for executing, did Prince Bagration save the military which even stayed in battling request. However, one couldn't neither depend on comparable uncommon conditions nor complete them as a rule.

Thus, Prince Bagration appreciated and noticed the circumstance like a genuine battleship. Be that as it may, let us return to issue at hand.

Armies: Napoleon and the Russians
Napoleon's military was very nearly 500,000 in number. He separated it into three principle parts. The Emperor himself along with the Guard and three infantry corps

under Davout, Oudinot and Ney, three cavalry corps under Nansouty, Lebrun and Grouchy, 250,000 men taking all things together, ready to assault the focal point of the First Army before it could effectively accumulate its powers. The King of Westphalia with the corps under Junot, Poniatowski, Reynier and Latour-Maubourg's Cavalry Corps, 80,000 men taking all things together, was to move against our Second Army. The Viceroy of Italy and the focal armed force, likewise around 80,000 men, comprising of the corps directed by Beauharnais and Saint-Cyr, were requested to assault between our two militaries and keep them from joining together. Moreover, the adversary had two flanking corps: on the left flank Macdonald with 30,000 was to enter Courland, undermining Riga and our right flank, and at the furthest edge Prince Schwarzenberg with the Austrian Corps additionally with 30,000 men held off Tormasov's Third Army. Yet, Napoleon, terrified of losing time and not meaning for the armed forces of the Viceroy of Italy and the King of Westphalia to enter with him in a solitary line, started to cross the Niemen inverse Kovno on twelfth June.

Our militaries were conveyed in the accompanying way: the First Western

Army, numbering up to 127,000 men was sent from Russia to Lida. The base camp were in Vilnius. The Second Western Army was little with 40,000 men and took up positions from the town of Mosta up to Pruzhany. The central command were in Volkovisk.

he Third Western Army of around 25,000 men stretched out from Lyuboml' to Stary Konstantinov. Its central command was in Lutsk.

Napoleon's Crossing of the Niemen. The retreat of the First Army
We learnt of the foe's intersection of the line on the evening of twelfth June. The First Army was requested to focus behind Vilnius. General Platov was requested to start his activity against the adversary's flank, and Prince Bagration was requested on thirteenth June to build up Platov while thinking about the past orders not to lose correspondence with the First Army. Sovereign Bagration was put in a most troublesome situation: by building up Platov, he needed to progress and accordingly would have to break all contact with the First Army.

After disclosing this to the Minister of War on fourteenth June, he rather mentioned authorization to go through Bialystok and Ostrolenko to Warsaw with General Platov's Corps and the Second Army, which would represent up to 40,000 men under arms. Anticipating consent either to build up Platov or to

retreat to Minsk, or maybe staying enthused about his arrangement to attack Poland, Prince Bagration stayed set up until eighteenth June. However, this error went to the Army's benefit. Assuming the Second Army had withdrawn on the fourteenth to get together with the First Army, then, at that point, it would have either found Marshal Davout's Corps, or, in the wake of signing up further toward the north with the Army of General Barclay de Tolly, the two armed forces would have been cut off from Smolensk, driven north, and afterward every one of the assets of the southern regions would have been in the adversary's hands. From the start of the mission Napoleon didn't comprehend the topography of Russia well; however as of now at Smolensk every one of his moves were guided towards pushing us toward the north. In the mean time on the sixteenth Prince Bagration got a message from the Minister of War that the First Army was withdrawing to Sventsyany. Platov was requested to follow them there, and Prince Bagration to endeavor something very similar, so the foe would not remove his street through Minsk to Borisov.

The Retreat of the Second Army
Thus, the Second Army started its retreat on eighteenth June behind the Shchara. Around the same time in Zelva Colonel Benckendorff conveyed a request that the Second Army should walk toward Novogrudok to Vileika to get together with the First Army. On the 22nd the Army showed up in Novogrudok. That very day spans were worked across the Niemen in Nikolaev and five Cossack regiments crossed. Here Prince Bagration discovered that Davout, despatched from Vilnius, currently involved Olshany, Volozhin and Vileika, was all the while progressing and, therefore, remove his way. Along these lines he had to alter course and retreat as beforehand to Minsk. Making progress toward Minsk we got news that the adversary previously showed up around here. This was on 25th June. The hotness was agonizing. The men were totally depleted from 40-and 50-verst walks on sandy ways. It was difficult to constrain a forward leap. Ruler Bagration chose to withdraw not to Minsk, but rather through Nesvizh, Lutsk to Bobruisk. The military showed up at Nesvizh on 26th June. Ruler Bagration was faulted for this retreat to Nesvizh. Nonetheless, he was totally defended in doing as such given the tactical contemplations. He saw that over all he needed to protect his Army and that the intersection with the First Army the named way was outlandish, on the grounds that Davout was before him with 50,000, and behind him the King of Westphalia followed with 80,000 men. In this manner on eleventh June (from Slutsk) Prince Bagration even chose to keep in touch with the Emperor that to sign up his Army when General Barclay de Tolly was withdrawing further toward the north, to the Drissa camp, was

scarcely to our advantage, on the grounds that the adversary could generally defeat us on our left.

Platov's cavalry skirmishes at Korelichi, at Mir and at Romanov
From Nesvizh the genuine retreat started in sight of the foe. Platov, withdrawing from Grodno to Novogrudok and Strakhovichi towards Nesvizh, got together with the Second Army by these methods. He had 10 regiments, representing under 4,000 men, however in this situation they were more helpful than 10 regiments of customary cavalry. The Cossacks glanced around all over, they knew it all and under the administration of Platov they battled surprisingly. On the 26th the foe showed up at Korelichi from the bearing of Novogrudok as three sections of rangers. One Polish regiment was excessively energetic as they moved toward our vanguard and was nearly destroyed by Ilovaisky and Karpov's regiments. General Platov withdrew to

the town of Mir. At sunrise on the 27th three regiments of Polish uhlans[5] showed up under the order of General Turno. Platov had his own style of war. Seeing the foe, he partitioned his separation into a few sections dependent on the conditions. He concealed one to the right, one more to the left, and the rest of show up before the adversary, once in a while propelling, then, at that point, withdrawing, to bait and direct him along these lines onto the flanking snare. Then, at that point, in the wake of striking at the adversary in the flank and the back, he sought after and annihilated them in case they were in jumble. Assuming they hung on tenaciously and it was difficult to conquer them forcibly, the Cossacks would disperse to and fro and get together again at an assigned point. This was by and large what Platov did in this occurrence. Three regiments of uhlans were totally obliterated. General Turno scarcely got away with his life. We were left with in excess of 400 detainees, including two lieutenant-colonels.

Meanwhile Prince Bagration sent General Vasilchikov and the Akhtyrsky Hussars, Kharkov Dragoons and one infantry regiment to help Platov. Towards the evening General Platov, following the Army's developments, withdrawn behind the town of Mir. Trusting that after this example the Poles would leave him in harmony, during the night he really focused as normal on the advantage of the ponies and men and stayed close to the stream, without intersection to the next bank, and intersection with the infantry alone. On the morning of the 28th the high level posts, arranged five versts away, educated him that the adversary rangers was assaulting them in power. This was the Polish division of General Rożniecki, the vanguard of the King of Westphalia. General Platov himself saw the adversary and requested his men to search for portages. The riverbed was made

of dirt, they took the ponies and didn't track down any passages. There stayed just a little wooden scaffold to make the intersection. Platov said: "Relax, chaps," and chose to battle. He, at the end of the day, sat in the brambles at one roadside. Ilovaisky stow away in the other, and left just two regiments before the foe. Six regiments of uhlans hurled themselves forward and as regular entered excessively far up to the actual extension. Platov struck against the flanks; the undertaking was drawn out, and from the start nobody knew how it would end. Nonetheless, the foe was overwhelmed by the consolidated powers of the Cossacks and the Akhtyrsky Hussars. Out of the entire Polish division, where there were up to 4,000 men, after the fight close to 1,200 were left. Up to 600 fell into our bondage, the rest were killed.

Platov sought after Rożniecki for in excess of 10 versts, and the adversary general was just saved by connecting up with the fundamental powers of the King of Westphalia.

This fight extraordinarily affected resolve. In the mounted force one is either continually destroying the foe, or one is continually being beaten. Everything relied upon the principal achievement. Platov needed to overcome the foe at Mir to stop the brags and boldness of the Poles. Our rearguard was assaulted indeed at Romanov, yet the first mounted jaeger[6] and one grenadier regiment completely
bliterated the adversary, and consequently after this the Army as of now not heard anything of the alleged fearsome Polish cavalry, which Napoleon had up to 20,000. His vanguard previously halted their interest, and just held the Second Army under perception. Right now Napoleon, disappointed by the King of Westphalia for his powerless interest, moved the order of his powers to Marshal Davout.

Retreat to Bobruisk
Prince Bagration, proceeding with his retreat, shown up at Slutsk on first July, where he got news that the foe (a piece of Davout's Corps) was at that point found in the town of Svisloch on the Berezina 40 versts upstream from Bobruisk. This stronghold was the main place of retreat for the Second Army. We needed to possess it before the foe. Ruler Bagration sent Raevsky's Corps to Bobruisk to assault the foe, disregarding the numbers and the sustained position, yet Davout went directly to Minsk, and we involved Bobruisk unopposed. Here we discovered that Davout's Corps reached out from Minsk to Orsha. Ruler Bagration requested VII Corps to stock just up on hardtacks in Bobruisk and to rush to Mogilev by constrained walks, to arrive before the foe. It was hard to track down constrained walks, for example, those during the retreat of the

Second Army in the records of military history. We walked 45 to 50 versts a day.[7] The horrendous hotness, sand and absence of clean water additionally depleted the men. There was no time even to cook porridge. During this time the positions lost 150 men. At the top of the section with the 26th Division, luckily, I had a huge inventory of rolls and vodka. Permitting the men a twofold portion,
this upheld the warriors, yet in spite of this I lost 70 men from the ranks.

At Stary Bykhov we discovered that the foe had as of now taken Mogilev.

Colonel Sysoev ventured out in front of VII Corps with three regiments, that is with 1,000 Cossacks. The Corps continued towards Dashkovka. Sysoev moved toward Mogilev and got together with Colonel Gresser's unit of 300 men, which the foe had driven from the city. Toward the start of the mission Gresser was in Borisov and withdrawn to Mogilev.

ysoev's cavalry skirmishes at Mogilev

While withdrawing, Sysoev baited the foe to follow him. The adversary cavalry here messed up the same way that it had recently made against Platov. The best regiment from Davout's vanguard approached. Sysoev totally demolished it, sought after the escaping men up to the actual entryways of the city and caught 300 detainees along with their colonel. Sysoev said that he was requested to get hold of them by the tongue. He figured out how to get hold of their whole regiment. The foe regiment had up to 800 men in the positions. Moreover there were up to 200 Poles present. In this way, 1,000 Cossacks crushed 1,000 of the French armed force's best normal cavalry.

We gained from the detainees that there was an infantry division and a rangers division in Mogilev and towards the evening they were anticipating part of another infantry division. By the way, the divisions in Davout's Corps each included 20 units toward the start of the mission. Toward the start of the conflict there were 1,000 men in each brigade. As of now the regiments were comprised of five brigades of up to 850 men in each; however Davout shaped exceptional units from the grenadier and rifle regiments and subsequently had seven contingents every one of 600 men in each regiment. Along these lines, he had 28 regiments in a division against our 12. These numbers clarify why an adversary division could battle against one of our corps, which had 24 regiments each.

n Dashkovka something happened which showed how vital an illustration of discipline was around then. The soldiers were remaining in their positions.

Suddenly I heard an awful commotion and cry in the town. It worked out that our soldiers were mindful and specifically the men of the Orel Regiment. I requested them to assemble and rebuffed the last ones to show up in their places. This model had an incredible impact, and starting here the Orel Regiment caused less trouble.

The Battle of Saltanovka

On the evening of tenth July VII Corps got a request from Prince Bagration to lead a surveillance mission in power. Sovereign Bagration got insight that there were simply 7 to 10,000 adversary assembles Mogilev. Hence, the Prince requested us to assault them and possess the city in their stead. General Raevsky took with him the sixth and 42nd Jaeger Regiments from the twelfth Division, and two brigades from my 26th Division. I chose one legion from the Orel Regiment, and one more from the Nizhny Novgorod Regiment, and requested them to leave behind their backpacks so they could move quicker. Promptly toward the beginning of the day of the eleventh we started to assault. There was a distance of around five versts among us and the adversary. At one and a half versts we met their infantry vanguard and drove them free and clear. The gunfire expanded in force gradually, and both jaeger regiments were occupied with activity while moving toward Saltanovka. The adversary pulled out to its positions. At nine o'clock the cannon shots rang out during the Second Army's first significant commitment in the 1812 campaign.

Marshal Davout, expecting an assault on his position, arranged his guards ahead of time. The extension at Saltanovka was blockaded and weapon provisos were removed of the dividers of the hotel, arranged on the left bank of the gorge and securing the whole French line. The extension at the factory of Fatova was broken and provisos were additionally cut into the adjoining houses. Three legions were positioned at Saltanovka, one force at Fatova, supported by five different legions behind it, four regiments were positioned among Fatova and the town of Seltso, while two additional brigades were positioned by the gorge before this last town. The entirety of the rangers, comprising of the Cuirassier Division of General Valence, General Chastel's Light Cavalry Division and one regiment of mounted chasseurs from General Bordesoulle's unit, were for possible later use behind the conservative past the town of Seltso out and about driving from it to the town of Starye Buinichi. Five contingents were conveyed further to one side, by the town of Zastenke, lastly the last five units were sent before Mogilev.

Marshal Davout's infantry comprised of two regiments from Compans' Division, comprised of 25 brigades; his cavalry power was comprised of 48 groups. Notwithstanding this the adversary anticipated support from the unit of General Pajol and the Polish Vistula Legion, however these soldiers would just get together with him after the fight. Sovereign Bagration, without exact data about the foe's solidarity and speculating that he had close to 6,000 men against him, sent his auxiliary with a request for General Raevsky to gather every one of the men in his Corps and strikingly assault the French position and take Mogilev. General Raevsky sent for his leftover soldiers. Since the backpacks of two regiments of the 26th Division were abandoned, the other two units needed to convey them. They showed up just toward the finish of the fight. In this manner the 26th Division toward the beginning had just eight regiments while the twelfth had ten forces. The whole Corps comprised of five regiments of the 26th Division, three regiments of the twelfth Division, twenty units of mounted force, three Cossack regiments and 72 guns.

When the soldiers were accumulated, General Raevsky requested me to lead my Division, three regiments of Cossacks, the Akhtyrsky Hussar Regiment and to walk towards the adversary's flank. General Raevsky expected that I would outmaneuver the adversary's conservative, since it was a verst from the street. While I would pass on the forest to level ground and do an assault from the flank, he expected to hit at the middle with the twelfth Division.

arrying out the request, I took order of Colonel Sysoev's Cossacks, who battled in a similar spot three days prior, and drove my powers left for the defeating move. Woods stretched out across this whole region. I should progress along the way which wound between the trees three men wide.

In the forest I experienced our marksmen in confusion, withdrawing from the French skirmishers. The foe was defeating our left along a similar street. The musketeers from my driving contingents halted the foe and overran them. I requested to seek after them to the edge of the forest and followed with the excess powers. The top of my section was comprised of contingents of the Orel and one Nizhny Novgorod force, behind them 12 weapons, then, at that point, the Poltava [Poltavsky] Regiment, six additional firearms and the Ladoga [Ladozhsky] Regiment with the other Nizhny Novgorod brigade, two firearms, lastly, the cavalry.

Leaving the forest, I found the shooters who were completing my request by the edge of the woods trading discharge with the foe, lying behind a little rise before the town of Fatova. Behind them I saw the shimmering knifes of two French sections. The distance between them was close to 60 sazhens.[8] The thick woods didn't permit me to return my men into
segment development. Progressing to one side in separations, leaving the forest if conceivable, I was obliged to set up a front by the edge of the forest. The terminating proceeded. To collect companies, I needed to walk forward until I was 30 sazhens from the foe. Colonel Sysoev was likewise here.

Only two legions were stretched out in line, I requested Colonel Ladyzhensky to assault the foe with a yell of "hurrah", to seek after them up to the waterway and overwhelm the extension. Then, at that point, subsequent to possessing the main houses on the contrary bank, to anticipate my orders. The foe was authoritatively overwhelmed at that point and escaped more than 150 sazhens from the extension. Seeing that the legions were crossing the extension, I moved 12 firearms to the statures and requested the Poltava Regiment to continue similarly to the far bank under the front of this battery. Subsequent to setting up the mounted guns, I watched out from the statures to see who I was battling. The adversary's infantry remained in two lines from the fundamental street to the actual wood. The cavalry was conveyed in a third line.

Moving six additional weapons to the battery and putting the Ladoga Regiment on the left flank, I advanced toward the right flank. I was astonished to find that the foe shooters who were dug in there in the gorge had increased their fire. Our big guns, losing men and ponies, was removed from the position. I built up them. In the interim I saw that the Poltava Regiment was withdrawing and their colonel was injured. I requested the regiment to stop, I rode further, hoping to meet the Orel and Nizhny Novgorod units, I saw two legions leaving the wood in the back of my position. I rode dependent upon them, yet incredibly I saw French grenadiers at just 30 speeds. They were instructed by Colonel Achard. The French sought after our legions and were nearly at our rear.

Fellows, forward!" I shouted out to the Poltava

Regiment. They hesitated.

"Hurrah! Fix blades!"

They didn't move.

From the positions I heard a voice: "If by some stroke of good luck the

mounted guns were with us." "Great," I said, "hang on here."

I rushed to the gunnery, sorting out behind my position a battery of four weapons, gotten back to the Poltava regiment and driven them to the cannons. The adversary, seeing their retreat, flooded forward with the cry "en avant!"

The regiment terminated, and canister struck the French forces. They halted and were tossed into confusion.

I rode up to the Poltava Regiment and provided the request "advances!" They hurried advances and pursued the foe up to the scaffolds. There my pony was injured by two bullets.

The Poltava Regiment was in jumble. I just barely figured out how to stop it and send it back to the edge of the forest. However, to seem more grounded to the adversary troops, they were framed in line and seemed, by all accounts, to be a solid segment. With the men expanding their pace of discharge twofold, I requested every one of the 18 weapons to start shooting at the adversary segments. The impact was amazing to the point that I perceived how they were continually moving about and evolving places, removing themselves from me and from additional canister shot. Their misfortunes were critical. At last, they withdrew, multiplied the pace of mounted guns discharge and the commitment was drawn.

I will take this second to clarify why our soldiers withdrew. The Nizhny Novgorod and Orel units, after at first tossing the adversary back and crossing the extension, involved the hotel and a few houses in the little town on the opposite side of the stream. They had quite recently settled control and were leaving the little town when four French contingents, lying in the rye, showed up at 30 sazhens, terminated a round and accused of blades. The different sides occupied with hand to hand battle. The French hurried at the white norm of the Orel Regiment and held onto it from the fallen leading figure. Our sergeant grabbed it back from the French, yet was himself killed. The standard was lost once more. Indeed it was taken by us, and amidst the battle the shaft was broken. As of now an assistant of the Orel Regiment raced into the conflict, gotten the norm and conveyed it from the battle. Colonel Ladyzhensky was injured in the jaw and fell. A big part of our two contingents were lying dead or injured. They had to withdraw and were driven back to the forest. Two contingents sought after them. We set up a

battery and traded fire for mutiple and a half hours.

At this second I heard weighty fire to one side. This was General Raevsky, assaulting the foe's position head on. The forest encompassing the town of Saltanovka didn't permit us to move toward it by some other means than the principle street, along which the foe battery was positioned. Toward the stopping point the scaffold was as yet blockaded. The Smolensk Regiment of the twelfth Division pushed ahead with inconceivable determination, yet couldn't catch the extension. Officers Raevsky and Vasilchikov surged before the sections yet the predominance of the adversary's position discredited every one of the bold endeavors of our fighters. They couldn't break into the town and the fire of the foe battery was focused out and about. In the interim while trading fire with the adversary, I sent a report from my area to General Raevsky, illuminating him that I experienced on the left flank not 6-, but rather maybe 20,000 men. Subsequently, assuming we needed to overcome them, I would should be sent a few brigades as fortifications. General Raevsky answered that his assaults were repelled, that he lost numerous men and subsequently couldn't send me more than one battalion.

It was around four PM. My soldiers were at that point depleted. Just the rangers was as yet not locked in and this was simply because the lush landscape didn't permit me to utilize it. I took the legion of the 41st Jaeger Regiment which was shipped off me and continued through the forest past the adversary's right flank. I requested Colonel Savoini to cross the extension at Fatova and assault the French with blades while simultaneously I would arise free and clear and assault the enemy.

To our left side flank I found Colonel Ladyzhensky with a Nizhny Novgorod contingent, which was occupied with extraordinary fire across the stream. I arose out of the edge of the forest inverse the town of Seltso and was at that point one and a half sazhens from the adversary line when General Raevsky's auxiliary showed up with a request to withdraw. He said that Commander-in-Chief Prince Bagration, in the wake of showing up among the twelfth Division face to face, was persuaded that there were not 6-but rather in excess of 20,000 foe assembles front of them. Be that as it may, it was badly designed for us to retreat.

It was nearly evening. I could hang on until sunset. Withdrawing along the lush way in sight of the foe and being so near them, I could be overpowered by them. The aide answered that General Raevsky had effectively removed with the twelfth Division and sent just this request. There was

nothing else to do. I needed to get back with the unit of the 41st Jaeger Regiment and found my situation before the town of Fatova in a similar condition as I left it. Leaving behind the brigade of the 41st available for later, I requested Colonel Savoini to hang on as in the past, and by and by went with General Raevsky's auxiliary determined to persuade the Commander-in-Chief to stay in position until sunset.

pon appearance, I found neither Prince Bagration nor General Raevsky. I could see that the twelfth Division was in full retreat and the musketeers currently totally abandoned the backwoods. I observed just the divisional officer General Kolyubakin who was meandering among the soldiers carelessly. General Vasilchikov was additionally here. Realizing that Kolyubakin was a torpid individual, I went to Vasilchikov and said that in case they were not to hang on until dusk, then, at that point, not to fail to remember that the soldiers of the 26th Division stayed more than 500 sazhens ahead and that assuming the twelfth Division didn't stand by, and would proceed with its retreat and forsake the forest, then, at that point, I would be driven out behind the entirety of my ordnance to save the men. I requested that he stay in the forest until I joined the line. Vasilchikov at first answered that he was not the senior official, but rather I signaled to Kolyubakin, and he chose to provide the orders himself.

asilchikov ended the soldiers, provided the order "advances!" and here I got a show of the soul and discipline of the Russian fighter in the entirety of its power. The soldiers charged at the adversary, overran them and indeed involved the forest. I jogged towards my men to put together the retreat. To withdraw at 100 sazhens from the adversary, who partook in every one of the benefits of territory, was a troublesome task.

Meanwhile in my nonappearance Savoini by and by got the request to withdraw, yet he answered that he was unable to settle on the choice without me. I showed up and right now observed two legions conveying their backpacks. Appending the 41st Jaeger Regiment to them, I gave the accompanying attitudes: the infantry should frame squares in echelons and take their positions while going through the forest, in the mean time all the ordnance in my Division should consolidate and twofold the power of fire. The two infantry regiments – the Ladoga and Poltava – would involve the edge of the woods.

fter permitting time for the soldiers to get coordinated, I requested the cannons to pull out their weapons in pairs beginning from the flank, leaving two firearms on

the street by the entry to the forest, while the rest would go through the forest drawn by ponies. The musketeers were informed that when the last two weapons were removed, they would themselves fall back and take up position at the edge on the flanks of the ordnance. Everything was conveyed precisely in a specific order. The adversary, seeing this incidental retreat, charged head on at our men, however here they were met with canister from the two weapons and the shoot from two infantry regiments. The foe stopped and we went through the forest so effectively that I didn't lose a solitary gun.

ehind the forest there was a clearing and a town 500 sazhens away. While in the clearing I put the regiments in line, coordinated a battery and when the remainder of our musketeers left the forest and the foe started to show up, I started shooting from the battery's firearms in general. Here I observed that the twelfth Division had kept up with its position and was in a solitary line with me. We kept on withdrawing, covered by rangers on our flanks, and involved the statures we found behind us. The barrage didn't stop. The foe halted at the kickoff of the forest. Around evening time we continued to our past position toward Dashkovka. Here we remained for the entire day of twelfth June. The foe didn't show up. In the interim scaffolds were worked at Novy Bykhov. To cover our developments toward this path, Prince Bagration requested General Platov (who got a request to get together with the First Army) to get over the Dnieper at the portage at Vorkhalabov with 12 regiments around evening time, seeming to assault Mogilev from the contrary side, and afterward to continue further to the First Army nearby between the Dnieper and Sozh rivers.

The retreat through Mstislavl to Smolensk
At sunrise on the thirteenth we walked to Stary Bykhov. On the fourteenth we crossed the scaffold at Novy Bykhov and went through the night at Propoisk.

Prince Bagration was worried about the possibility that that the foe would arrive at Mstislavl before him, yet we didn't experience them there, and on the seventeenth we showed up at Mstislavl and proceeded unhampered making a course for Smolensk. We owed this to the Battle at Saltanovka. In spite of the fact that Marshal Davout got fortifications in the night after the fight and had his whole Corps available to him, he didn't walk out of Mogilev yet invigorated the city with dug in batteries. The fight at Mogilev significantly affected him. He actually recognized that he never saw such a persistent infantry engagement. The enemy lost up to 500 killed, 500 in captivity, and more than 3,000 lay wounded in the Mogilev hospital. On our side up to 3,000 men were also taken out of action. The battalions which were at the head of the columns lost half their strength.[9] There remained around 250 men in each of these battalions. Here I learned how savage battles are against regular troops, and especially against the French army of 1812.[10]

The great retreat of our military even with Napoleon's significantly unrivaled numbers fills in as undisputed evidence of the prevalence of the Russian soldiers. In the commitment around Mogilev (at Dashkovka and Saltanovka) 20 of our units, numbering under 11,000 men, assaulted 20,000 French infantry [16 battalions], clutched the situation for the entire day, and their mental fortitude gave us the glad result that the adversary was restricted in Mogilev and started to dig in themselves rather than beating us to Mstislavl. Subsequently, they permitted us to join the two western militaries in Smolensk. The whole Second Army was obligated to its Commander-in-Chief Prince Bagration. He realized how to rouse us with a feeling of power. Additionally, every birch tree remaining by the roadside advised us that we were battling in Old Russia. We spilled our blood on all of them. The injured officials, even the warriors, in the wake of having their injuries dressed, rushed to return again to their places.

The junction at Smolensk
The Second Army, leaving Mstislavl on nineteenth June, shown up at Smolensk unrestricted on the 22nd and set up camp before the city. The First Army had as of now been there from the twentieth and was sent on the right bank of the Dniepr. The two armed forces stayed for quite a while under the dividers of Smolensk. Here we were supported by seventeen regiments from the disbanded corps of General Baron Wintzingerode. The Second Army got seven contingents, and hence we by and by had 500 men in a unit. Together both armies

accounted for 120,000 available men. In the First Army there were 77,000,[11] and the Second 43,000. But a detachment under Major General Neverovsky, consisting of the 27th Infantry Division and the Kharkov Dragoon Regiment, around 7,000 men in all, was detached from the Second Army. Prince Bagration ordered them to occupy the town of Krasny. While we were at Smolensk nobody thought that the city could be fortified. Meanwhile we could only use the old walls, improve the earthworks and build new field fortifications on the left flank of the city. Since the enemy headquarters were in Vitebsk, we expected that they would assault us from that side. However, Napoleon had something different as a main priority. He definitely knew, as we would in this manner see, that in case he had the option to drive us out northwards, then, at that point, the conflict would be chosen in his favour.

A chamber of war was brought in Smolensk. Notwithstanding the two presidents, the participants incorporated His Imperial Highness Tsesarevich Konstantin Pavlovich, the Chief of Staff of the First Army Major General Ermolov, the Chief of Staff of the Second Army Saint-Priest and Quartermaster General Colonel Toll. Colonel Toll at first recommended to exploit the hole between the French corps, reaching out from Vitebsk to Mogilev, by assaulting the focal point of their brief quarters, subsequent to progressing the majority of our powers towards the town of Rudnya. Albeit at first we planned to anticipate the adversary under at Smolensk and to do these manners appropriately, yet in the interim we got news that the foe was progressing with the Corps of the Viceroy of Italy with rangers against our right flank, and the choice was made in accordance with to Colonel Toll's idea to proceed to assault him, on the conviction that Napoleon's whole armed force was there.

At sunrise on 26th July, the Russian armed force walked out in three segments. The First Army represented the two segments on the right, the Second Army the one on the left. The central command of General Barclay de Tolly was moved to Prikaz-Vydra and Prince Bagration's to the town of Katan. On the 27th we got news that all the adversary progressed posts had withdrawn. General Barclay expected that Napoleon planned to bypass his right flank close to Porechye, and in this way chose to stop the walk to Rudnya and stretch out further to one side. On the 28th the central command of the First Army moved to the town of Moshchniki. The Second Army supplanted it at Prikaz-Vydra. On 30th June Prince Bagration showed up on the left bank of the Dniepr by the town of Rosasny. He was worried that the unit of Major General Neverovsky, left behind in Krasny, may be crushed if the French showed up in Smolensk before the Russians, and chose to withdraw under the dividers of the city. On 31st June the central command of the Second Army moved to Smolensk. In the mean time General Barclay de Tolly got news that the foe had left Porechye. In any case, he was worried about his right flank and took the choice to proceed with the walk to Rudnya.

On first August the base camp of the First Army was moved to Shelomets.

The Second Army was requested to walk to Nadva. Sovereign Bagration left Smolensk with VIII Infantry Corps and showed up at Katan on the second, and at Nadva on the third. VII Infantry Corps was to follow Bagration one day later.

All these walks first and foremost to Rudnya, then, at that point, to Porechye and again to Rudnya nearly caused the annihilation of our militaries by opening up our passed on flank to the adversary and the principle street to Smolensk. Napoleon, when he discovered that the Russian armed force was walking to Rudnya, quickly exploited the error of the Russian commanders. Subsequent to gathering every one of the powers on his right flank, he chose to outmaneuver our left, get over the Dneipr [... to take Smolensk in the back of our militaries, driving them north to Velike Luki or Toropets and to separate them from the focal areas of Russia.

Fortunately, in the evening of third August Prince Bagration got a report from General Neverovsky that the adversary was crossing the Dnieper in enormous numbers][12] at Rosasny and Khomino and progressing towards Krasny. The Commander-in-Chief arranged him to hang on to the extent that this would be possible. VII Corps, which previously walked to Katan that day, was requested to get back to Smolensk,
o through the city and rush to Neverovsky's guide. General Raevsky requested me to take eight contingents of the 26th Division and structure his vanguard, to progress similar to Krasny. Going through Smolensk, I experienced a few trumpeters and the kapellmeister of Kharkov Dragoon Regiment, who let me know that there was a fight at Krasny, that the 27th Division hung on valiantly, however was totally crushed that main a few trumpeters figured out how to get away. Realizing that we needed to battle at Smolensk, I checked out the dividers of the city. Riding further, after three versts I met General Neverovsky's aide and five weapons which were saved from the foe rangers. I gained from the auxiliary that Neverovsky really lost a large portion of his men, yet withdrew all neat and tidy and was six versts away. I before long met him. He told me the following.

General Neverovsky's retreat
The foe assaulted him at Krasny. Neverovsky, seeing that there was a prevalent power against him, left behind a solitary jaeger unit in Krasny, and with the remainder of his men took up a position three versts behind the town, covered by a gorge. The foe assaulted the city with the total of his rangers and, to his adversity, just a single battery and an infantry division. Our

men were driven out of Krasny, and the unit withdrew to our position. Neverovsky had 12 battery weapons and two horsedrawn firearms from the Don Cossacks. He confined the two horsedrawn firearms with one contingent of infantry, sending them 12 versts not too far off to Smolensk, and requested them to possess the intersection of a little waterway streaming past there, while he framed up his own division, set the battery weapons on the left flank, securing them with the Kharkov Dragoon Regiment, and conveyed the Don Cossack regiment on the right flank. Neverovsky admitted that assuming he had put the battery between the infantry sections, then, at that point, the mishaps that were to occur for him would not have taken place.

he adversary had 15,000 mounted force which flanked around our left. The Kharkov Dragoon Regiment, seeing the assault, charged forward themselves, yet was invaded and sought after for 12 versts. Then, at that point, the battery was left without security. The foe hurried at it, overran the position and caught five firearms, while the excess seven pulled out along the Smolensk Road. The Cossacks likewise neglected to stand firm on their situation. Hence, from the earliest starting point of the fight Neverovsky was left without cannons, without rangers, with the infantry alone. The adversary encompassed him on all sides with their cavalry. The infantry assaulted from the front. Our soldiers hung tight, repulsed the assault and started to withdraw. The adversary, subsequent to seeing the retreat, increased their rangers assaults. Neverovsky quit for the day infantry in segment and was covered by the trees which lined the street. The French cavalry was continually rehashing its assaults at General Neverovsky's flank and back, ultimately requesting his acquiescence. He declined, and the men of the Poltava Regiment who were with him on that day, shouted out that they would bite the dust however not give up. The adversary was entirely close, to the point that they could converse with our troopers. On the fifth verst of the retreat the French dispatched their greatest invasion, yet the trees and trenches in the street forestalled them to cut up our columns.

The perseverance of our infantry invalidated the savagery of their assault. The adversary perpetually brought new regiments into the commitment, and every one of them were beaten back. Our soldiers, without regimental differentiation, accumulated into a solitary segment and withdrew, terminating back and repulsing the assault of the adversary cavalry. Subsequently Neverovsky withdrew for another seven versts. At a certain point a town nearly annoyed his retreat, since they were halted there by birch trees and trenches in the street. To try not to be totally destroyed, Neverovsky had to leave behind piece of his soldiers, which were then

cut off. The rest of while battling. The foe arrived at the back of the segment and continued close by it. Luckily, they had no gunnery, and along these lines they couldn't annihilate this small bunch of infantry. Neverovsky was at that point moving toward the waterway, and when he was a verst away, the two weapons which he had sent there recently started shooting. The foe imagined that there held up a solid Russian support, severed from our back, and our men securely crossed behind the waterway. Here they hung on until the evening. In the night they withdrew one more 19 versts up to the gorge which was 6 versts from Smolensk, where I thought that they are on the 3rd.

On this day our infantry covered itself with greatness. One should make reference to that it was a humiliation for the French to have just a solitary battery with 15,000 rangers and an infantry division. In case they had their whole gunnery with them, then, at that point, Neverovsky would have died. Nor did their cavalry do themselves much honor, for 15,000 of them couldn't obliterate 6,000 of our infantry.

f one looks at the French armed force all the more intently, whom we were without a doubt used to being in stunningness of, then, at that point, we would see that their commanders were not really talented as our rivals needed us to accept, and their cavalry was undeniably less deserving of the recognition that they credited to themselves. The genuine benefit of the French during the mission of 1812 was simply the impressive predominance in numbers.

apoleon was exceptionally disappointed with the attitudes of his commanders on that day. "I had expected," he said, "the whole Russian division, and not the five firearms which you have brought with you."

Smolensk

On third July, at seven AM, I gotten together with Neverovsky and educated him regarding the Corps officer's structure to move order of the vanguard to me, and for him to get together with the Corps. My soldiers took up position behind the gorge. At four PM the principal adversary flanking units showed up, trailed by the vanguard. The foe mounted force, subsequent to overpowering my Cossacks, moved toward the gorge and were halted by the gun discharge from my battery. On the opposite side of the statures the adversary shaped up in fight request. Their solid segments turned once they were level

with my flank. I saw that up to 4,000 cavalry outmaneuvered me on the left and halted in the town. Sunset shut down every one of these manoeuvres.

Preparations for the Battle of Smolensk

At 12 PM I got a request from the Corps officer to go to his base camp. He was positioned with the twelfth and 27th Divisions three versts behind my position and a similar separation from Smolensk.

I found General Raevsky who was encircled by his commanders. "Ivan Fyodorovich," he said to me, "we have gotten a request to hang on until the last limit, to give time for the military to get to Smolensk. I have picked this position and we have chosen to get fight here."

I replied, "And you will be totally beaten. Assuming anybody is saved by fortune, then, at that point, essentially we will lose every one of our weapons, and critically, Smolensk will be in the possession of the enemy."

Raevsky grinned: "For what reason do you think so?"

You involve a similar situation as mine, three versts before you. The right flank is guarded by the Dniepr, however the left flank is totally open. Also, there is an empty behind you through which the gunnery can't pass. Today the adversary mounted force circumvented my left flank. Tomorrow it will rehash a similar move against you. Assuming you are additionally beaten back by the French from the front, then, at that point, during the fight they will outmaneuver you on the left and take Smolensk. You will be compelled to withdraw and have the disaster to pull out towards your left flank, under the control of the adversary. Remember that there is a gorge behind you, and there are the dividers of Smolensk. Assume that you were to hit at the foe with your infantry, and under the most ideal situation you even advance back to suburbia of Smolensk, yet you can't bring your artillery."

Where do you figure we should give fight?" Raevsky asked me.

"In Smolensk itself. Maybe we will hang on there. Even from a pessimistic standpoint we will lose the big guns, however we will save the Corps. Regardless, we will win time and offer the military the chance to go to our aid."

General Raevsky fell into profound idea. It was hard for him to leave his arrangement to battle on a position he had picked, and on second thought to acknowledge another outer assessment, and albeit this depended on a more prominent likelihood of

achievement, we stayed peacefully. At last, to alleviate him from this abnormal position, I welcomed him to mount up, since the night was twilight, to assess Smolensk and pick more favorable territory where he could convey the soldiers in case of fight. General Raevsky agreed.

Smolensk lies on the left bank of the Dniepr and is encircled by high stone dividers. The dividers were outfitted with 30 pinnacles. The dividers were encircled by a shallow trench and before it a covered way with a glacis. On the statures on the western side of the city there was an enormous earthen stronghold of an unpredictable shape which was known as the Royal Bastion. Suburbia were arranged on the left side. However, every one of the earthen fortresses had fallen on the grounds that Smolensk was totally deserted. There stayed just the stone dividers, very much safeguarded except for one side, confronting the waterway, where there was an imploded segment of around 50 sazhens. Along the street I said to General Raevsky: "Permit me to show you where we can battle easily."

He answered that he comprehended everything and concurred with my perspective. I encouraged him to permit me and the 26th Division to involve the Royal Bastion, whereupon, no doubt, the foe would focus on his assault. Raevsky requested the soldiers of the twelfth Division to involve the left suburb. Then, at that point, the infantry was requested to withdraw, and the rangers was left set up until additional thought. It was to keep its pit fires consuming and pull out to Smolensk when the foe assaulted it. During the night I involved myself with the demeanor of the soldiers. I set two firearms on the right flank, covering the street along the Dniepr, I put six legions from my Division to cover the street. I introduced 18 weapons on the stronghold and dissipated the men of the Vilnius [Vilensky] Regiment on the divider. Colonel Stavitsky's unit from the 27th Division, which had gone under my order, remained at the burial ground of the left suburb while 24 firearms were set before the graveyard. Eight forces and 24 firearms of the twelfth Division were in the actual suburb with the request to burn down the houses and retreat into the city in case the adversary were to assault suburbia in strength. At last, there were two forces and four firearms on the left flank, and available for later the excess unit of the 27th Division. Having laid down a good foundation for ourselves thusly, we anticipated the appearance of the foe. Around six AM I went to sleep.

he Battle of Smolensk

After half an hour I was awakened. The enemy had already appeared. Our cavalry retreated from the enemy with all its agility. We opened fire from the guns and stopped their pursuit. Less than 20 minutes passed when we saw three large columns of French infantry, shortly thereafter Napoleon himself was spotted among them.[13] One of the columns headed straight for the stronghold, the second to the graveyard, the third along the Dniepr, to our right flank. I accused of the six brigades lying available for later and drove them through the uncovered way. Every one of the seventeen of our weapons were at that point in real life. Yet, the foe walked past the shells and the canister and was moving toward the canal of the post of Smolensk which appeared as a chasm. I had quite recently figured out how to arrange one legion when the French were on the glacis. The Orel Regiment opened rifle shoot and halted the foe's development. A few times the foe attempted to escape the gorge, a few times they hurried at our infantry, however every time they experienced our weighty fire and had to get back to the gorge. Their bodies covered the glacis. After seeing that the adversary assault was wavering, I requested the first force of the Orel Regiment to accuse at them of bayonets.

The contingent left the covered way, yet stopped after seeing that the second brigade was not after behind them. I dispatched my aide Borodin. He remained on the glacis a few speeds from the foe, shouted out "Hurrah!" and the two forces repeated his cry as they charged at the French. In the interim the Ladoga and Nizhny Novgorod Regiments assaulted with blades and conquered the adversary, who were driven away from the chasm while their bodies cleared the whole region from the glacis up to the contrary side of the gorge. My regiments charged after the foe. I sounded the review, brought them back and by and by shaped the legions behind the covered way. Before long the foe got fortifications and moved toward us indeed, yet they halted on the contrary side of the gorge and traded fire, not setting out to charge us anymore.

On the left flank the adversary moved toward our batteries in wedges and sections and climbed their own cannons. They were met with canister. General Raevsky, scared of losing the firearms, requested them to pull out, however the leader of one of the mounted guns organizations Lieutenant Colonel Zhurakovsky chose to wait and kept on shooting canister. Before long there followed an overall cry of "hurrah", and the adversary was spurned on this side with critical misfortunes. There were no assaults on the left suburb where the twelfth Division was stationed.

All this occurred at around nine AM. As of now the whole French armed force started to think under the dividers of Smolensk, took up their positions and encompassed the city. I saw up to 200,000 men here, remaining in dull masses. The foe, seeing the bombed assaults, set up a battery and started to fire at the dividers of the city, supporting the holes between the batteries with infantry in wedged developments. Whole regiments drew closer by unit and dissipated into wedge development. We lost not many men behind the covered way, yet the French continually supported their legions. We had terrible guns. I requested the men to gather up French black powder rifles and substitute them for the entire regiment.

At around late morning our Second Army showed up on the contrary bank. Sovereign Bagration, subsequent to dispatching General Raevsky on the earlier day, expected to cross the Dniepr at the town of Katan himself, yet after finding that every one of Napoleon's powers were coordinated towards Smolensk, obliterated the scaffold and set out from Katan at dawn on the fourth. VII Corps was supported by the second Grenadier Division of Prince Karl of Mecklenburg. I was sent a contingent of the Siberian Grenadier Regiment. Towards the evening General Barclay de Tolly showed up with the First Army which remained on the statures of the right bank of the Dniepr. At this point I saw that the two armed forces were set up in their positions. Napoleon had 185,000 men under arms, not including Junot and the Viceroy of Italy's Corps, who didn't figure out how to interface up with them. On our side we scarcely had 130,000 men. The blast proceeded with into the evening. Our Commander-in-Chief showed up and expressed gratitude toward me for this commitment, accepted me and said: "I know, Ivan Fyodorovich, what you have achieved, I realize that we are obligated to you." I was excited. Practically the entirety of our officers came to perceive how the glacis inverse my stronghold was covered with the assortments of Frenchmen. At last, the Minister-Commander likewise came dependent upon me and expressed gratitude toward me with his trademark coolness.

VII Corps, depleted by the multi day walk and fight, was supplanted by VI Corps during the evening of the fifth. The great decision of landscape was demonstrated by General Barclay de Tolly's structure for VI Corps to take up the very same positions which VII Corps had involved, and overall to complete similar attitudes which were executed on the 4th.

Napoleon wrote in his journals: "He [Napoleon] turned the left of the Russian armed force, crossed the Dniepr and moved toward Smolensk, where he showed up 24 hours before the Russian armed force which had been confined during its retreat. One division of 15,000 Russians which turned out to be in Smolensk had the fortune to protect this spot for a day which gave Barclay de Tolly an opportunity to show up on the next day. Assuming that the French armed force had overwhelmed Smolensk, it might have crossed the Dniepr and assaulted the Russian armed force in the back while it was in jumble and not yet rejoined. This great

opportunity would be missed."[14]

Both presidents feared being outmaneuvered at Elnya and to lose correspondences with Moscow. They accordingly chose to stretch out further to one side. General Barclay de Tolly assumed liability for the guard of Smolensk, and Prince Bagration for the insurance of the Moscow Road. On fifth August, at four AM, the Second Army set out and took up its situation on the Moscow Road behind the Kolodnya River eight versts from Smolensk. He left behind its rearguard four versts from the city inverse the jail of the town of Shein, which remained toward the finish of the French right flank. General Raevsky and the soldiers under his order connected up with the Second Army except for the 27th Divison and two regiments of the twelfth (the sixth Jaeger and Smolensk), which stayed in Smolensk. I was additionally requested by General Raevsky to remain behind to coordinate the activity. "Since I," he said, "coordinated every one of the procedure on the 4th."

My soldiers were supplanted by Major General Likhachev's 24th Division. In the wake of sending his division, I rode to the Corps officer General Dokhturov and thought that he is in the strongholds before the entryways of Smolensk. In the wake of paying attention to me, he requested me to relate this to his boss from staff. In the wake of tracking down Colonel Monakhtin, I saw that he had disbanded an entire detachment which supplanted my soldiers and set them in wedge arrangement coordinated at the foe under his battery. They had no stores. His arrangements may be invaded, and the adversary may go into our strongholds along with our men. In the wake of telling Monakhtin the manner by which we did the guard on the fourth, I returned and met General Konovnitsyn at the doors, who was himself attempting to track down me. Not knowing me, he inquired: "Would you say you are General Paskevich? We have been requested to gain from you."

We rode around Smolensk, and for over an hour I let him know all that had occurred on the fourth in the best detail. I was glad to see this general, who was the main one to raise the matter and needed to know every one of the subtleties. Maybe appropriately on the fifth, when in the occasion the seventh Division was overwhelmed and needed to escape, General Konovnitsyn realized how to arrange the entire issue, making a move with his division against the adversary, and shut down any further attacks. Then, at that point, I additionally saw General Count Kutaisov. He pulled out the 24 weapons which I had set up in the burial ground with the understanding that the firearms were not secure there. Yet, these 24 firearms covered the empty, and without them the adversary could assault the left suburb without any problem. In the occasion this occurred. At the point when Napoleon coordinated his I Corps against the suburb toward the start of the fight, the foe went through the hollows and took the flank of the seventh Division and nearly obliterated it throughout the span of thirty minutes, and there Konovnitsyn himself left the city in the nick of time and halted the enemy.

n the fifth General Dokhturov safeguarded Smolensk with the two divisions of his Corps, the 27th Division under General Neverovsky, the third Infantry Division under General Konovnitsyn and two regiments of the twelfth Division. During the day he was supported by another division under Prince Eugen of Wurttemberg. Dokhturov lost suburbia, however hung on in the city. Be that as it may, despite our bold guard, Smolensk was presented to risk on a few events, particularly when Napoleon sent his Polish Corps from the right flank to the back of the city, where the divider was obliterated in one place.

We had not many men and barely any weapons in this area. The Poles might have effortlessly gotten through, yet their fortitude was deficient. They were at that point 100 speeds from the rubble and pulled out. I was astonished to see that General Barclay de Tolly had possibly positioned 24 firearms on the flanks when he might have sent 100 of them. Then, at that point, there would have been lower hazard and less misfortunes of men. I was certain that for this situation we might have clutched Smolensk for the third day, on the grounds that the foe had as of now lost around 15,000 men in these two days. Napoleon was entirely disenchanted, to the point that he set up enormous batteries to crush the dividers of Smolensk, like he could obliterate them with field firearms. Around five o'clock Smolensk was totally overwhelmed on fire. Obviously, it was precarious to clutch the city once correspondences with the flanks from inside the post were compromised. Yet, it was believed that the fire may stop, and afterward the adversary sections could progress into the city with difficulty.

Two days under the dividers of Smolensk had cost Napoleon around 20,000 men. Sovereign Bagration, knowing the tenacious willfulness of the Emperor of the French, was sure that he would restore his assault on the next day and by and by lose as numerous men. Thusly during his gathering with General Barclay de Tolly at around two o'clock he requested that he hang on in Smolensk. Then, at that point, he dispatched to him an assistant with a letter to this end. In the First Army the II and IV Corps and the Grenadier Division were at that point presently not in real life. It followed, maybe, for them to supplant the five divisions of VII Corps, and hold the city for one more day. In any case, General Barclay de Tolly accepted that Napoleon, by stretching out further to one side, could catch the Moscow Road and that the Second Army was not in a condition to protect it. Under this supposition the evening of the sixth Barclay and the First Army didn't just pull out from Smolensk, yet additionally the Petersburg suburb, staying on the Petersburg Road and subsequently withdrawing himself from the Second Army, which stretched out to the Soloviev crossing on the Dniepr.

At dawn, following the developments of our soldiers the foe crossed the Dniepr at a passage, caught the Petersburg suburb and cut General Barclay off from the Moscow Road. Konovnitsyn had to return and drove the French out of the suburb, yet he lost in excess of 1,000 men in the process.

The First Army took up its situation headed straight toward Porechye. The Second continued to Dorogobuzh, leaving behind a rearguard on the Smolensk Road under Major General Karpov with four Cossack regiments.

We withdrew from Smolensk in sight of the foe troops. First the rangers showed up, then, at that point, the infantry. They set up a battery, and we pulled out under their fire. However, after six versts they let us be. In the interim the situation of the First Army making progress toward Porechye, as I previously referenced, by and by isolated it from the Second Army. It needed to get onto the Moscow Road to get back to its normal flow of action.

General Barclay de Tolly committed an error by staying on the Petersburg Road for a day and a half, and just doing the move during the evening of the third day. It was hard to gain ground through the terrible back roads. Additionally a solitary minor yet heartbreaking episode made them cover just six versts during the whole evening. The driver of an ammunition truck nodded off and tumbled from his pony. The section stopped, kept the soldiers following behind it, and hence deferred the walk until sunrise. The corps in the First Army were dispersed and just barely tried not to be cut off from the Moscow Road.

The Battle of Valutina Gora broke out unequivocally because of this heartbreaking occasion. The First Army must be given opportunity to get onto the Moscow Road, along which the adversary was seeking after General Karpov's rearguard meanwhile. Significant General Tuckhov, dispatched with 2,400 men to build up Karpov, experienced the high level sections of Marshal Ney's Corps and from ten AM until three PM he opposed the attack of the mathematically predominant foe power. During this time fortifications continued to move toward the foe. Slowly our soldiers additionally came nearer. Toward the finish of the fight the French had up to 35,000, while we just had 16,000 men. This was a sublime day for Russian arms. The Commander-in-Chief General Barclay de Tolly himself drove contingents on pike charges on a few events. The unrivaled steadiness of our infantry, specifically the grit of the first Grenadier Division, and Adjutant-General Count Orlov-Denisov's splendid mounted force assaults fill in as additional evidence of the prevalence of the Russian army.

The French credited the disappointment of their attack on that day to the error of General Junot, who was apparently incapable to get around our left flank, however I imagined that this move was not even imaginable because of the swamps. During our retreat from Valutina Gora the Poles tracked down the chance to show their ill will towards us. They killed injured Russian detainees in our sight. On ninth August the Second Army showed up at Dorogobuzh. The First advanced toward the town of Usvyaty on the River Uzha. General Barclay de Tolly, indeed getting together with the Second Army and reestablishing interchanges with the Second Army, needed to stop and anticipate the adversary. In any case, at Usvyaty the mathematically predominant adversary could defeat our left wing, cut us off from Dorogobuzh and drive us into a corner at the juncture of the Uzha and Dniepr streams. Ruler Bagration persuaded General Barclay de Tolly to withdraw along the way to Vyazma and track down another prevalent position. Be that as it may, in the environs of Vyazma there were no adequately great situations for the fight to come. The two militaries proceeded with their retreat and on the seventeenth showed up at Tsarevo-Zaymishche. On that day General Miloradovich showed up in Gzhatsk from Kaluga with a corps of 15,000 recently enlisted troops. With this support General Barclay de Tolly indeed needed to anticipate the adversary at Tsarevo-Zaymishche, yet his arrangements for the fight to come were by and by halted by the appearance of General Prince Golenishchev-Kutuzov who was designated Commander-in-Chief of all Russian militaries battling Napoleon.

Fortunately, in light of this we didn't persevere at the situation at Tsarevo-Zaymishche. The level vast field would have been to the upside of the solid foe mounted force, which dwarfed our own by 25,000 men.

Borodino

Kutuzov's arrangement as president of the multitude of armed forces Kutuzov's appearance raised the soul of the Russian armed force. The Commander-in-Chief needed to exploit the demeanor of the soldiers and do Barclay de Tolly's aim to give fight to the adversary. In the event that one couldn't expect a conclusive triumph, then, at that point, essentially it would be feasible to incur upon the foe misfortunes which he was unable to renew. In any case, before that General Kutuzov needed to connect up with Miloradovich's Corps. In addition, as I have effectively said, the situation at Tsarevo-Zaymishche was totally open and was not to our advantage.

In Mozhaisk Kutuzov met General Bennigsen, who, being without an order, was leaving the military. Subsequent to designating him Chief of Staff of his military, Kutuzov requested him to distinguish appropriate ground for the fight to come and Bennigsen picked the Borodino field. On nineteenth August the Russian armed force went through Gzhatsk and got together with Miloradovich's Corps at the town of Ishakova. On the twentieth the military walked to the town of Durik. On the 21st we continued to the Kolotsky religious community and on the 22nd the army took up[15] the position near the village of Borodino which had been chosen for the battle.

General Konovnitsyn was left with the rearguard at the Kolotsky cloister. On the 24th he was assaulted by the foe's vanguard and made a courageous stand, however withdrew and enlisted in the military whenever he was defeated by the Viceroy of Italy's forces.

The right flank of the situation at Borodino was close to a wood, a large portion of a verst from the Moskva River. The Kolocha River, moving through a profound ravine,

covered the front of the traditional and the middle up to the town of Borodino. The left wing reached out from the Borodino statures to the hedges which were to one side of the town of Semenovskoye. The front of the left wing was just to some degree protected by a couple of gorges and bushes.

This position was artificially strengthened. The woods on the right flank were protected by separate fortifications.[16] A battery was established in the centre upon an elevation in front of village of Gorki, through which the main road passed. Another battery was placed 200 sazhens in front, towards the village of Borodino. The most vulnerable piece of the position was the left flank which in this manner required solid fortresses. There, where the middle got together with the left flank, an enormous battery was built on the statures which investigated the field before the left wing, as a lunette with a fractional drapery divider along the sides.[17]

Three more batteries were established at the end of the flank on the heights in front of the village of Semenovskoye.[18] The village of Semenovskoye was gutted. Jaegers were dispersed among the bushes in front of the line on the left wing. Finally, in order to observe the enemy's movements against the left flank a redoubt was developed by the town of Shevardino 900 sazhens before the line.

n 24th August the foe, subsequent to driving Konovnitsyn's rearguard out of the Kolotsky cloister, moved toward Borodino in three sections. Shoot from the redoubt at Shevardino and marksmen in the towns of Fomkino and Aleksino annoyed the foe's right flank. This constrained them to endeavor to take the redoubt.

[We saw that a mass of rangers was slipping from the statures inverse us. Two commanders rose up out of this mass. One was in a dim jacket and a cornered cap. For fifteen minutes he noticed our position, waved his right hand, and after 30 minutes inferno down-poured to our left side flank. In this quarter of an hour Napoleon sorted out the shortcoming in our position. In this assault he utilized the aggregate of his I Corps and his Polish Corps, around 50,000 men.

There begun][19] the most stubborn struggle. Three times the redoubt changed hands. But as it was built only to observe the movements of the enemy and was so far from the army's main position, it could not be defended successfully, and at ten o'clock in the evening our troops were withdrawn and the redoubt was left in the possession of the enemy.

While the French were assaulting Shevardino on the 24th, they were likewise assaulting my left flank. I sent two jaeger regiments with 12 weapons into the shrubs around the stream, and along with the excess two regiments of my Division I progressed to support the jaegers. They hung on until the evening and the foe couldn't beat my jaeger unit. Albeit the greater part of Colonel Zhuravsky's 12 weapons were made an out of move and in some measure a large portion of the ponies were lost, the ordnance didn't withdraw. The commitment cost me up to

800 men, and my pony was injured by a bullet.][20]

n the 25th Napoleon, guaranteed that the most fragile area of our position was the left flank, gathered his powers in the middle and on his right flank. Kutuzov, seeing this attitude and scared of being outmaneuvered on the left along the Old Smolensk Road, dispatched Lieutenant-General Tuchkov with III Infantry Corps, 7,000 men of the Moscow state army and six Cossack regiments to the furthest limit of the left wing. General Tuchkov's men were sent behind the town of Utitsy. The space among them and the left flank of the primary position was involved by four jaeger regiments. The remainder of the soldiers were positioned in the accompanying way. The fortresses before the town of Semenovskoye, toward the finish of the left flank, were shielded by General Vorontsov's Division. The 27th Division of General Neverovsky remained behind him in the subsequent line. Behind the town of Semenovskoye Prince Karl of Mecklenburg's Division was conveyed in two lines. VII Infantry Corps reached out between the town of Semenovskoye to the primary battery. My 26th Division was in the bleeding edge. Count Sivers' IV Cavalry Corps was set available for later of VII Corps.

The whole left wing was monitored constantly Army and was under the order of Prince Bagration.

okhturov's VI Infantry Corps involved the focal point of the situation from the right flank of Raevsky's Corps straightforwardly inverse the town of Borodino up to the battery before the town of Gorky. The right flank was involved by Count Ostermann's IV Infantry Corps, bordering its passed on wing to Dokhturov's Corps. Noble Korf's II Cavalry Corps remained behind him, lastly Baggovut's II Infantry Corps, who framed the super right of the military before the sustained woods on the position's right flank. The right flank under the order of General Miloradovich, who along with General

Dokhturov were under the order of Barclay de Tolly.

General Uvarov's I Cavalry Corps was set for possible later use on the conservative behind the forest. Platov and nine Cossack regiments were to one side. The excess five Cossack regiments remained by the juncture of the Kolocha and Moskva streams, keeping watch along the banks.

General Duka's second Cuirassier Division, behind Prince Karl of Mecklenburg's Division, framed the save of the left wing. The primary save, sent behind the middle, comprised of V Infantry Corps and the first Cuirassier Division under General Depreradovich. Five organizations of pony gunnery remained behind IV Cavalry Corps. The primary ordnance save of 180 weapons was arranged before the town of Pisarevo. The cutting edge, particularly on the left wing, was guarded by amazing batteries. All the jaeger regiments were ready to pounce among the bushes, towns, debases past the front line.

Meanwhile the foe made the accompanying dispositions.

Poniatowski's Corps was conveyed behind the shrubs to one side of the Shevardino redoubt and entrusted with defeating General Tuchkov's separation. The King of Naples and three cavalry corps were among the actual shrubberies. Marshal Davout was to assault the left half of the Russian left wing with three infantry divisions and remained between the town of Shevardino and the forest around the town of Utitsa. Marshal Ney was requested to lead his Corps and Junot's Corps to assault the right half of our left wing. His position stretched out from Shevardino to Aleksino. The Viceroy of Italy with his own four divisions, Grouchy's Cavalry Corps and Gerard and Morand's infantry divisions, remained inverse the middle. The position was strengthened with a few redans ignoring the town of Borodino. Our right flank was to be contained by Broussier's Division, the Italian Guard, Delzons' Division and Ornano's Cavalry Division. Napoleon's Guard was available for later to one side of the town of Fomkino. There were around 190,000 men[21] in the French army and up to a thousand guns.

The Russian armed force numbered up to 132,000. This included 115,000 normal soldiers, 7,000 Cossacks and 10,000 volunteer army. The big guns had 640 firearms available to its. In this position the two militaries went through the evening of the 25th to the 26th.

The Battle of Borodino

At six AM on the 26th August, a noteworthy day in the

chronicles of war, the bleeding fight started. Any kind of future family was advocated in considering this commitment the skirmish of giants.

Poniatowski was quick to progress, starting his activity to defeat Tuchkov's detachment.

hen Davout moved toward the entrenchments of our left wing. Simultaneously the Viceroy of Italy requested Delzons' Division to catch Borodino. The Guard Jaeger Regiment arranged a bold safeguard, yet had to leave the town and retreat behind the Kolocha River.

Meanwhile the commitment started on the limits of our left flank. General Tuchkov, under tension from Poniatowski, withdrew to a slope he found behind him and traded substantial fire with the adversary which proceeded until early afternoon. The corps under Davout, Ney and Junot and part of Murat's mounted force approached consistently and arranged straightforwardly inverse our batteries. Ruler Bagration, after seeing the adversary's mathematical prevalence inverse our left wing, requested Tuchkov to send Konovnitsyn's Division to help Voronstov and Neverovsky. Then, at that point, the second Cuirassier Division was additionally shipped off the left from the town of Semenovskoye. At long last, Prince Kutuzov at first sent the Izmailovsky and Lithuanian [Litovsky] Guard Regiments and a unit of grenadiers with two cannons organizations as fortifications, and afterward he requested the exchange of Baggovut's whole II Corps from the right flank to the left.

The enemy formed and advanced their columns under heavy fire from the Russian infantry and artillery. The enemy even managed to capture one fleche very quickly, but they were immediately overrun [by Count Vorontsov, whose Combined Grenadier Division charged with bayonets and drove the enemy backwards.][22]

In the middle the Viceroy of Italy left General Ornano on his right flank, involved the town of Borodino with Delzons' Division and set up batteries on the statures. In any case, they were quieted by our mounted guns a few times. Beauharnais himself crossed the Kolocha River with Morand, Gerard, Broussier's divisions and Grouchy's Cavalry Corps. In any case, here they met my shooters lying among the shrubberies through which the adversary needed to pass.

The French went through the brambles with the best of endeavors. For over an hour the jaegers from my Division kept down their development, and only

at ten o'clock was the adversary ready to drive back my sharpshooters and enter the gorge straightforwardly inverse our stupendous battery.

Broussier's Division descended into the ravine between the battery and the village of Borodino. [Morand and Gerard's divisions formed up in the same ravine and suddenly climbed out, preparing to attack the brigade on the battery, with the support of two more regiments behind them.][23]

Seeing that the foe was planning for an attack, I went out to meet them with the leftover regiments of my Division. I focused my jaegers and posted soldiers on the two flanks of the lunette, conveying the Nizhny Novgorod and Orel Regiments on the right hand side, the Ladoga and one legion of the Poltava on the left hand side. The men of other force of the Poltava Regiment were scattered across the stronghold and in the trench. The eighteenth, nineteenth and 40th Jaeger Regiments were put behind the lunette in reserve.

espite Russian ordnance fire, the adversary division progressed. In spite of the fact that we were dwarfed by the foe, I effectively held off the adversary's attack. At last, the prevalence of their numbers constrained me over pull out to change my drained regiments.

General Bonnamy's[24] 30th Line Regiment at the head of Morand's Division broke into our lines. He was supported by the entire division. But at this moment under the cover of the Ufa [Ufimsky] Regiment led by Count Kutaisov, I reorganised my Division again and charged at the enemy with the 18th Jaeger Regiment.

I review the horrible sight that showed up before me during the battle for the primary battery. The nineteenth and 40th Jaeger Regiments assaulted the foe from the left flank. General Vasilchikov and a few regiments of the twelfth Division fell upon them from the right flank. The 30th French regiment was totally obliterated. General Bonnamy was taken into captivity.[25] The rest of his regiment was driven back towards Morand's Division. I drove the leftover regiments of the twelfth Division, went behind the lunette to remove the French soldiers I found there. Built up by mounted force assaults, our incredible hostile showings tossed Morand's Division into chaos. The adversary's withdrawal in this area nearly caused his soldiers who had caught the town of Semenovskoye meanwhile to follow after accordingly. But

Beauharnais figured out how to support Morand with Gerard's Division and the battle was renewed.

Then we regained control of the lunette within a quarter of an hour. This struggle was one of the most terrible and bloody during the whole of the Battle of Borodino. The bodies of the enemy piled up in the lunette in front of the fortification. From our side General Konovnitsyn was killed.[26] A horse was killed from under me, and another wounded.

The Viceroy, neglecting to catch the lunette through the attack, strengthened the fire from his batteries against the stronghold and our soldiers. My Division, which had as of now lost close to a large portion of its men under the awful fire from the foe cannons which butchered entire columns of men, held fast with inconceivable boldness, as the actual French recognized. Showered with canister, it experienced such incredible setbacks that it had to pull out from the bleeding edge to be supplanted by General Likhachev's 24th Division, taken from the focal point of General Dokhturov's VI Corps.

But let us return on our left side flank. Marshal Ney and Junot's Corps needed to get through between the Russian left flank and General Tuchkov's soldiers, yet were beaten back by General Golitsyn's cuirassiers and Prince Eugen of Wurttemberg's Division. Poniatowski, helped by Ney's development, charged at Tuchkov and caught the kurgan to his left side flank. Tuchkov assembled every one of his powers, overran the Poles from the kurgan, yet was mortally injured himself. General Baggovut accepted his order. Napoleon provided requests to escalate the assault on the left wing before the town of Semenovskoye. The French assembled 400 firearms. From the Russian side there were 300 firearms in the batteries. Kutuzov likewise requested General Miloradovich to hustle there with the IV Infantry and II Cavalry Corps.

The fight by the town of Semenovskoye continued with another fierceness. The French assaulted. Accordingly Prince Bagration progressed his whole line with knifes. The attack was awful. Neither one of the sides needed to surrender the triumph. Sadly, General Bagration was injured. The French, after catching the fleches, charged at the Semenovsky gorge, yet were invaded by Konovnitsyn's Division, the Izmailovsky and Lithuanian Guard regiments and the cuirassiers. The French triumphs were ended further by the lucky rangers assault by General Uvarov on the right flank, which diverted

Napoleon's consideration. In any case, the adversary, subsequent to getting its left wing, arranged to

heighten the assault on the centre.

The Viceroy progressed towards the lunette with Gerard, Morand and Broussier's divisions, requested the mounted force corps under Caulaincourt (instead of the fallen Montbrunn) to assault the fortress between the town of Semenovskoye and the fundamental road.

General Barclay requested General Ostermann's IV Infantry Corps to supplant the essentially annihilated VII Corps. The Preobrazhensky and Semenovsky Regiments were sent behind them, and the II and III Cavalry Corps were called up from the reserve.

aulaincourt got through behind the lunette, encircled it from the back, yet was then killed, and his soldiers were put to trip by the regiments of Count Ostermann's IV Corps.

The Viceroy's infantry divisions assaulted the stronghold from the front. Likhachev's debilitated Division couldn't avoid for long. Likhachev was intensely injured and taken into bondage. Albeit the adversary additionally caught the lunette, the Russian militaries involved the statures behind the fortress and ended any further progress.

The last exertion in this well known day was done by Poniatowski who had caught the kurgan and driven General Baggovut to the statures by the wellspring of the Semenovskoye stream.

It was three PM. The adversary involved our principle battery and the fleches before the town of Semenovskoye, however his benefits were still insignificant.

These focuses were before the primary situation of the Russian armed force. Subsequent to withdrawing to the statures behind the Goritsky and Semenovsky gorges, they were no less forcing. To get a conclusive triumph, one needed to dispatch another attack against the whole line.

But the two militaries were similarly depleted and couldn't recharge their past efforts.

apoleon, scared by the horrendous illustrations learned by his soldiers, provided the request to stop the attack. Just the horrendous gun shoot proceeded until six o'clock in the evening.

At nine PM, the French by and by rose up out of the town of Semenovskoye and involved the gorge, yet were then defied by the Finland [Finlyandsky] Guard Regiment and crashed once again into the town. By dusk the French soldiers got back to the position which they involved toward the start of the battle.

Thus finished the Battle of Borodino, one of the most bleeding and generally renowned in the archives of military history.

The French misfortunes on that wicked day came to up to 60,000 men, including 20,000 killed and a greater number of than 1,000 captured.

The misfortunes on our side were no less critical. Up to 15,000 were killed, in excess of 30,000 injured, and around 2,000 men were taken into bondage. On that day Russia lost Prince Bagration, General Count Kutaisov, and Tuchkov.

Index of Names

Imperial Russian Army

Baggovut, Karl Fyodorovich (1761-1812). Baltic German infantry general in Russian help. Commandant of II Corps during the 1812 mission. Killed at the skirmish of Tarutino in October 1812.

Bagration, Pyotr Ivanovich (1765-1812). A Georgian sovereign, Bagration had a recognized military vocation and was one of the most well known officials in the Russian armed force. Bagration's own courage and hostile precepts were viewed as praiseworthy of the Russian armed force's best practices. In 1806 the court artist Gavrila Derzhavin hailed him as 'Lord of the military' (Bog-rati-on).
Mortally injured at the Battle of Borodino. In 1839 his remaining parts were reburied at Borodino at the foot of the primary landmark on the Great Redoubt.

Barclay de Tolly, Mikhail Bogdanovich (1761-1818). A relative of the

Barclays of Towie in Scotland who got comfortable the Baltic during the seventeenth century. Barclay filled in as Minister of War (1810-12) and was answerable for a progression of changes to set up the Russian military for war. He served Commander-in-Chief of the First Western Army in the 1812 campaign.

During the principal half of the mission Barclay and Bagration would differ passionately over vital decisions.

Benckendorff, Alexander Khristoforovich (1782-1844). An individual from the Baltic German respectable Benckendorff family, Alexander Benckendorff filled in as an administrator of a flying separation in the 1812 mission. Later in his vocation he acquired reputation as the top of the Third Department of the Imperial Chancellery, Tsar Nicholas I's mystery police.

Bennigsen, Levin August (Leonty Leontyevich, 1745-1826). Hanoverian cavalry general in Russian assistance. Bennigsen filled in as Commander-in-Chief of the Russian armed force against Napoleon in 1806-07. Kutuzov's Chief of Staff among August and October 1812.

Chichagov, Pavel Vasilyevich (1767-1847), a naval commander of the Russian armada who was named by Alexander I to order the Army of the Danube which had been recently connected with against the Ottomans. During Napoleon's retreat Chichagov was considered liable for permitting Napoleon to

escape at the Battle of Berezina. In 1813 he left Russia in shame and carried on with the rest of his life someplace far off, banished for good in France.

Depreradovich, Nikolay Ivanovich (1767-1843). Russian rangers general of Serbian beginning. Commandant of the first Cuirassier Division during the 1812 campaign.

Dokhturov, Dmitry Sergeyevich (1756-1816), administrator of VI Corps during the 1812 mission. Dokhturov's VI Corps saw broad activity at the skirmishes of Smolensk and Borodino.

Dorokhov, Ivan Semyonovich (1762-1815), head of the Isiumsky Hussar Regiment and administrator of the vanguard of Ostermann-Tolstoy's IV Corps. Following the Battle of Borodino Dorokhov filled in as a commandant of a flying separation working behind adversary lines.

Duka, Ilya Mikhailovich (1768-1830). Russian general of Serbian beginning. Officer of the second Cavalry Division's third mounted force unit, subjected to Bagration's Second Army. In August 1812 he took order of the second Cavalry Division following the demise of its administrator General Otto von Knorring.

Ermolov, Aleksey Petrovich (1771-1861). Head of Staff of Barclay de Tolly's First Western Army in the 1812 mission. Took order the big guns at Borodino following Count Kutaisov's passing. Later filled in as Russian emissary of the Caucasus being supplanted by Paskevich in 1827.

Ertel, Fyodor Fyodorovich (1768-1825), Prussian conceived official in charge of a different Reserve Corps toward the start of the 1812 mission. Ertel's Corps was subsequently subjected to Tormasov's Third Army.

Golitsyn, Dmitry Vladimirovich (1771-1844). Rangers general who was reviewed to military help by Kutuzov toward the finish of August 1812. Commanded the Second Army's mounted force with incredible qualification at Borodino.

Gresser, Aleksandr Ivanovich (1772-1822). A tactical designer, Gresser was elevated from colonel to the position of major-general toward the finish of 1812 for his activities at the Battle of Smolensk.

Ilovaisky, Nikolay Vasilyevich (1773-1838). Cossack general and individual from the unmistakable Ilovaisky family who later filled in as Ataman of the Don

Cossacks. As twelve individuals from the Ilovaisky family filled in as officials in the 1812-14 missions, Nikolay Vasilyevich is recognized from his family members in Russian sources as Ilovaisky-5.

Karpov, Akim Akimovich (1767-1837). Cossack general who directed the Second Army's Cossack separation during the Battle of Borodino.

Kolyubakin, Pyotr Mikhailovich (1763-1832). Commandant of the twelfth Infantry Division in Raevsky's VII Corps. Kolyubakin got a substantial injury at Saltanovka and didn't take part in the Battle of Borodino.

Konovnitsyn, Pyotr Petrovich (1764-1822). Commandant of the third Infantry Division in General Nikolay Tuchkov's III Infantry Corps. At Borodino Konovnitsyn briefly took order of the Russian left after Bagration's injury. Supplanted the mortally injured Tuchkov as officer of III Corps. Later filled in as Minister of War (1815-19).

Konstantin Pavlovich, Tsesarevich and Grand Duke (1779-1831). Fabulous Duke Konstantin was the more youthful sibling of Tsar Alexander and main beneficiary possible to the high position. He was in charge of V (Guards) Corps, prior to being shipped off St Petersburg by Barclay de Tolly for defiance. Later filled in as Viceroy of Poland and rejected the privileged position after the demise of Alexander I.

Korf, Fyodor Karlovich (Friedrich Nikolai Georg von, 1773-1823). Individual from Baltic German respectable family. Korf told the II Cavalry Corps in the First Army. During the Battle of Borodino he additionally directed the III Cavalry Corps.

Kutaisov, Aleksandr Ivanovich (1784-1812). Child of Tsar Paul's beloved Ivan Kutaisov. The youthful Count Kutaisov was a capable gunnery general and was by and large commandant of the ordnance at 28 years old. A famous figure in court circles, he was killed at Borodino in the wake of driving a counterattack close by General Ermolov to retake the Great Redoubt.

(Golenishchev-)Kutuzov, Mikhail Illarionovich (1745-1813). A veteran of Polish and Turkish conflicts, Kutuzov had directed the unified armed force at Austerlitz in 1805. He was liable for marking the Treaty of Bucharest which finished the Russo-Turkish War of 1806-12. In August he was named Commander-in-Chief of all the Russian armed forces. He passed on of ailment in 1813

while on campaign.

Ladyzhensky, Nikolay Fyodorovich (1774-1861). Commandant of the second detachment in Paskevich's 26th Division. Experienced a genuine injury at Dashkovka and didn't get back to the field until 1813.

Likhachev, Pyotr Gavrilovich (1758-1813). Commandant of the 24th Infantry Division in Dokhturov's VI Corps. On the evening of the Battle of Borodino, Likhachev's Division supplanted the 26th Division on the

Raevsky Redoubt. During the French attack Likhachev was intensely injured and taken into French bondage. Delivered in December, he kicked the bucket of his injuries the
following year.

Mecklenburg-Schwerin, Duke Karl of (1782-1833). The third child of Grand Duke Friedrich of Mecklenburg-Schewrin, Duke Karl served in the Russian armed force as administrator of the second Grenadier Division in the 1812 mission. He was injured at Borodino and was subsequently elevated to lieutenant general.

Miloradovich, Mikhail Andreyevich (1771-1825), Russian infantry general of Serbian beginning. Toward the start of 1812 he was answerable for selecting a corps of 15,000 men in the territories around Moscow. At Borodino Miloradovich took order of the conservative. Miloradovich's showiness procured him the epithet "the Russian Murat." As Governor General of St Petersburg, Miloradovich was killed during the Decembrist Uprising in 1825 as he endeavored to haggle with the rebels.

Monakhtin, Fyodor Fyodorovich (1775-1812). Head of Staff of Dokhturov's VI Corps. In the wake of separating himself at Smolensk, Monakhtin drove two blade charges against the foe at the Great Redoubt and was genuinely injured all the while. While recuperating from his injuries, he discovered that Moscow had been given up to the foe and detached his wraps and soon died.

Neverovsky, Dmitry Petrovich (1771-1813), commandant of the 27th Infantry Division during the 1812 mission. Neverovsky's men observed themselves to be the objective of extraordinary foe attacks at both Smolensk and Borodino. Neverovsky was mortally injured at the Battle of Leipzig in 1813. In 1912 his remaining parts were localized from Halle in Germany and reinterred on the Borodino battlefield.

Orlov-Denisov, Vasily Vasilyevich (1775-1843). Individual from a separated Don Cossack family, Orlov-Denisov was leader of the Life Guard Cossack Regiment during the 1812 mission. He partook in Platov's renowned rangers strike on the French left at Borodino.

Ostermann-Tolstoy, Aleksandr Ivanovich (1770-1857). An individual from the separated Tolstoy family and main beneficiary of the Baltic German Ostermann family, Ostermann-Tolstoy directed IV Corps for a large part of the 1812 mission. His soldiers shielded the Russian place on the evening of the Battle of Borodino.

Platov, Matvei Ivanovich (1753-1818), General of Cavalry and Ataman of the Don Cossacks. Platov filled in as administrator of the Cossack 'flying corps' during the 1812 mission and drove an attack around the French left at Borodino which occupied Napoleon for two hours and gave the Russian armed force significant chance to put together its defences.

Raevsky, Nikolay Nikolayevich (1771-1829), officer of VII Corps during the 1812 mission. VII Corps saw exceptional activity both during the retreat to Smolensk and at the clashes of Smolensk and Borodino. At Borodino Paskevich's 26th Division, some portion of Raevsky's Corps, guarded the Great Redoubt, otherwise called the Raevsky Redoubt.

Saint-Priest, Emmanuel de (1776-1814), French aristocrat who entered Russian help following the unrest. Filled in as the Chief of Staff in Bagration's Second Army prior to being intensely injured at Borodino.

Savoini, Geronimo (Eremey Yakovlevich, 1776-1836). Italian-conceived general in Russian assistance. Savoini told the Ladoga Infantry Regiment, one of four line infantry regiments in Paskevich's 26th Infantry Division.

Shcherbatov, Aleksandr Fyodorovich (1773-1817). Rangers general and individual from the august Shcherbatov family. He at first held an order in the Second Army however during the 1812 mission his units were moved and he was answerable for the arrangement of two rangers regiments.

Sivers, Karl Karlovich (1772-1856). Individual from unmistakable Baltic German family. Sivers directed the IV Cavalry Corps in Bagration's Second Army in 1812. He later served in the Imperial Senate.

Stavitsky, Maksim Fyodorovich (1778-1841). Authority of the first detachment in Neverovsky's 27th Infantry Division, seeing activity in a few fights throughout the 1812 campaign.

Sysoev, Vasily Alekseyevich (1772—1839), commandant of a Cossack regiment who separated himself in a few commitment throughout the 1812 mission. Elevated to major-general in December 1812.

Toll, Karl Wilhelm von (Karl Fyodorovich, 1777-1842). Baltic German staff official who filled in as Quartermaster General of the First Army and ordinary members in the boards of war. Cost accordingly served in a similar job with liability over the entire army.

Tormasov, Aleksandr Petrovich (1752-1819), experienced cavalry general who instructed the Third Army, which was entrusted with ensuring the line with Austria. He later filled in as Governor General of Moscow.

Tuchkov, Nikolay Alekseyevich (1765-1812). The oldest of four siblings who filled in as officers in the Napoleonic Wars. Nikolay Tuchkov directed III Corps in Barclay de Tolly's First Army. At Borodino he drove a separation on the super left of the Russian position and was mortally injured during the commitment. His most youthful sibling Aleksandr Tuchkov
(1778-1812) was killed at Borodino driving a detachment in Konovnitsyn's third Infantry Division.

uchkov, Pavel Alekseyevich (1775-1858). The third of the four Tuchkov siblings who served in the 1812 mission. He directed a unit in Baggovut's II Corps. Directing the First Army's rearguard at Valutina Gora, Tuchkov was intensely injured and taken into imprisonment. He stayed a detainee until the spring of 1814.

Uvarov, Fyodor Petrovich (1769-1824). Rangers general and officer of I Cavalry Corps. Most popular for going with Platov on a strike around the French left at Borodino.

Vasilchikov, Illarion Vasilyevich (1776-1847), rangers general and leader of a unit of the twelfth Infantry Division, part of Raevsky's VII Corps. Vasilchikov took order of the twelfth Division after Kolyubakin was vigorously injured at Saltanovka.

Vorontsov, Mikhail Semyonovich (1782-1856). Administrator of the

Second Combined Grenadier Division in 1812 and a corps authority in the missions of 1813-14. The child of Semyon Romanovich Vorontsov, the long-serving Russian diplomat to Britain (1785-1806), Mikhail Vorontsov was instructed in Britain and later filled in as Governor of Odessa.

Wintzingerode, Ferdinand von (1770-1818). Individual from German honorable family, Wintzingerode partook in the Napoleonic Wars under the banner of the Austrian and Russian militaries. In 1812 he instructed a unique cavalry separation working behind adversary lines.

Wurttemberg, Duke Eugen of (1788-1857). German ruler and a cousin of Tsar Alexander I. Matured 24 of every 1812 and a significant general starting around 1805, Eugen presented with unique excellence as the administrator of the fourth Infantry Division, part of Baggovut's II Corps.

Zhurakovsky, Ivan (Dates obscure). Lieutenant colonel. Administrator of the 26th gunnery unit's 47th ordnance organization, part of Paskevich's 26th Infantry Division.

Zhuravsky (First name and dates obscure.) Colonel. Commandant of a big guns organization in the 1812 mission. Present at Smolensk and Borodino.

Grande Armée and Allies

Emperor Napoleon I (1769-1821). Conceived Napoleon Bonaparte in Corsica, Napoleon was a well known and fruitful general during the French Revolutionary Wars. Subsequent to getting back from Egypt, he took power in the Coup of 18 Brumaire in 1799 and filled in as First Consul of the Republic until 1804. Sovereign of France from 1804-1814 and March-June 1815.

Achard, Jacques (1778-1865), colonel in charge of the 108th Line Regiment of the third Infantry Division during the 1812 campaign.

eauharnais, Eugene de (1781-1824), Viceroy of Italy and Napoleon's stepson from Empress Josephine's union with Alexander de Beauharnais. Eugene directed the Army of Italy in Napoleon's missions. Eugene's Italians were important for IV Corps during the 1812 campaign.

Bordesoulle, Étienne Tardif de (1771-1837), authority of the second Light Cavalry Brigade, part of the cavalry unexpected in Davout's I Corps.

Bonaparte, Jerome (1784-1860). Napoleon's most youthful sibling, whom he named King of Westphalia in 1807. Jerome directed VIII Corps made up fundamentally of Westphalians and was provided generally speaking order of the Grande Armée's traditional, working against Bagration's Second Army. Jerome was scrutinized by his sibling for his dormant quest for Bagration and got back to his realm in June.

Bonnamy, Charles Auguste (1764-1830), leader of the third Brigade of Morand's first Division in I Corps. At Borodino his soldiers took the Great Redoubt interestingly yet were driven back by a savage Russian counterattack. Bonnamy was intensely injured and taken prisoner.

Broussier, Jean Baptiste (1766-1814). Commandant of the fourteenth Infantry Division, part of Eugene de Beauharnais' IV Corps in the Grande Armée. Partaken in the attack of the Grand Redoubt at Borodino.

aulaincourt, Auguste-Jean-Gabriel de (1777-1812). The more youthful sibling of Armand de Caulaincourt, Napoleon's Master of the Horse and previous French diplomat to Russia, Auguste de Caulaincourt was joined to Napoleons central command during the 1812 Borodino crusade. At Borodino he was requested by Napoleon to assume responsibility for the fallen Montbrun's 5th
Curassiers. The cavalry effectively caught the position however Caulaincourt was killed by a Russian cannonball.

hastel, Louis Pierre Aimé (1774-1826), officer of the third Light Cavalry Division in General Grouchy's III Reserve Cavalry Corps.

Compans, Jean-Dominique (1769-1845). A staff official in Napoleon's initial missions, Compans directed the fifth Infantry Division in Davout's I Corps. He battled at Smolensk and Borodino, and was injured in the last engagement.

Davout, Louis-Nicolas (1770-1823), Marshal of the Empire and one of Napoleon's most skilled authorities. Nicknamed the Iron Marshal, Davout is most popular for his triumph over the vitally Prussian armed force at the Battle of Auerstedt in 1806. Davout instructed I Corps in the 1812 campaign.

Delzons, Alexis-Joseph (1775-1812). Leader of the thirteenth Infantry Division in Eugene's IV Corps. Delzons' men were among the first to be

occupied with the Battle of Borodino. Delzons was killed at the Battle of Maloyaroslavets while driving a counterattack to retake the town from the Russians.

Gérard, Maurice-Etienne (1773-1852). Authority of a detachment in the third Division in Davout's I Corps. He expected order of the third Division following the passing of its authority General Gudin at Valutina Gora. He battled with unique excellence at Borodino and was subsequently elevated to divisional general.

Grouchy, Emmanuel de (1766-1847). Mounted force general in charge of the III Cavalry Corps in 1812. Cantankerous battled at Borodino and was genuinely injured during the mounted force commitment in the late evening. He took order of Napoleon's Sacred Squadron during the retreat from Moscow, a unit of officials shaped to secure Napoleon. He was the last broad Napoleon named as Marshal of France during the Hundred Days in 1815. He is most popular for being missing from the field at Waterloo.

Junot, Jean-Andoche (1771-1813). Confidant to Napoleon in 1793 and probably Napoleon's nearest friend in arms. Junot was set in charge of VIII Corps in the wake of King Jerome's re-visitation of Westphalia. He was censured by Napoleon and future antiquarians for neglecting to trap the Russians during their retreat from Smolensk. Junot's regularly sporadic conduct was ascribed to head wounds experienced in his childhood and he ended it all in 1813.

Latour-Maubourg, Victor de Fay de (1768-1850). Mounted force general at the top of the IV Cavalry Corps in 1812. Battled at Borodino and was injured during the battle.

Lebrun de la Houssaye, Armand (1768-1846). Mounted force general who directed the third Light Cavalry Division in Grouchy's III Corps in the 1812 mission. He was intensely injured at Borodino and taken prisoner by the Russians during the retreat.

Macdonald, Etienne Jacques Joseph Alexandre (1765-1840). The child of a Scottish fighter, Macdonald was named Marshal of the Empire in 1809 on the front line of Wagram. He told X Corps on the left wing of the Grande Armée in 1812.

Montbrun, Louis-Pierre (1770-1812). Mounted force general renowned for leading

the rangers charge at Somosierra in Spain. He told II Cavalry Corps in the 1812 mission. At Borodino he was struck by Russian gunnery shells before long the start of the fight and passed on a few hours later.

Morand, Charles Antoine (1771-1835). A veteran of the Italian and Egyptian missions, Morand was put in charge of the first Infantry Division in Davout's I Corps in 1812. He battled at Smolensk and was injured in the jaw at Borodino.

urat, Joachim (1767-1815). A swank mounted force authority and perhaps Napoleon's most punctual confidant in arms, Joachim Murat wedded Napoleon's sister Caroline in 1800 and was accordingly named King of Naples (1808-15). Murat told the cavalry save in the 1812 mission, which comprised of four corps. His standing for grit and his splendor on the front line procured him regard among the Russians, and a few Cossacks welcomed him to turn into their Ataman.

Nansouty, Etienne-Marie-Antoine Champion de (1768-1815). A rangers general in charge of I Cavalry Corps in Murat's mounted force save during the 1812 mission. At Borodino he was injured in the knee.

Ney, Michel (1769-1815). An alluring cavalry officer, Ney was perhaps Napoleon's most punctual marshal in 1802. His III Corps battled fearlessly at Borodino and Napoleon conceded Ney the title of Prince de la Moskowa.
During the retreat Ney's men were encircled yet figured out how to circumvent, procuring him the epithet the Bravest of the Brave.

Ornano, Pierre-Antoine d' (1784-1863). A cousin of Napoleon, Ornano told the cavalry unforeseen in Eugene's IV Corps in the 1812 mission. His activities at Borodino won him advancement to the position of divisional general.

Oudinot, Nicolas Charles (1767-1847). Marshal of France beginning around 1809 and commandant of II Corps in the 1812 mission. Oudinot's men were requested to walk on St Petersburg however Oudinot was injured at the Battle of Polotsk and surrendered his order to Gouvion St-Cyr. Oudinot is known to have been injured multiple times in his military career.

Pajol, Pierre-Claude (1772-1844), brigadier general and authority of the rangers in Davout's I Corps, later leader of the second Division of II

Cavalry Corps. Battled at Borodino and was genuinely injured at Mozhaisk days after the fact while seeking after the withdrawing Russian army.

Poniatowski, Józéf Antoni (1763-1813). Clean sovereign and nephew of King Stanislaw II August Poniatowski, the last King of Poland. In 1812 Poniatowski instructed V Corps in the Grande Armée which generally comprised of Polish soldiers. He instructed the Grande Armée's right flank at Borodino. He was subsequently made Marshal of France by Napoleon during the Battle of Leipzig, the main non-Frenchman to appreciate such a qualification, yet was intensely injured during the French retreat and suffocated in the River Elster while endeavoring to escape.

Reynier, Jean (1771-1814). A gifted Swiss official who directed the VII Saxon Corps during the 1812 mission. Reynier's Corps partook in tasks against Tormasov's Third Army and didn't partake in the significant skirmishes of the campaign.

Rożniecki, Aleksander (1774-1849), Polish mounted force general who directed the fourth Light Cavalry Division in Latour-Maubourg's IV Cavalry Corps during the 1812 mission. Following the foundation of the Congress Kingdom of Poland in 1815 he entered the help of the Imperial Russian Army and filled in as the top of the mysterious police in Poland.

Gouvion Saint-Cyr, Laurent (1764-1830). A capable general who in 1812 was in charge of VI Corps, principally comprised of Bavarian soldiers. His Corps was disengaged to help Marshal Oudinot's walk on St Petersburg. He took order of the left wing after Oudinot was injured and scored a strategic triumph at Polotsk in August. Napoleon granted him a marshal's mallet in acknowledgment of the victory.

Schwarzenberg, Karl Philipp von (1771-1820). Austrian general who was exceptionally regarded by Napoleon and directed the Austrian helper corps during the 1812 mission. Schwarzenberg's Austrians assumed a minor part in the battling. The next year Austria joined Russia and Prussia in the Sixth Coalition against Napoleon and Schwarzenberg was named Supreme Commander of the united armies.

Turno, Kazimierz (1778-1817), Polish brigadier general who directed the 29th Light Cavalry Brigade, part of Rożniecki's Division.

Valence, Jean-Baptiste Cyrus de (1757-1822). Authority of the fifth Cuirassier Division, part of General Nansouty's I Reserve Cavalry Corps.

Notes and Commentary

[1] The previous Orel Regiment was reformed into the 41st Jaeger Regiment. (author's note)

[2] Imperial Russian unit of measurement corresponding to 1.07 kilometres.

[3] The Orel, Nizhny Novgorod, Poltava and Ladoga Infantry and the 5th and 42nd Jaeger Regiments (author's note)

[4] Part of the Russo-Turkish War (1806-1812).

[5] Uhlans were Polish light cavalry units armed with lances.

[6] Jaegers were light infantry units armed with rifles, used for skirmishes and screening line infantry units. Mounted jaegers would ride into position on horseback, dismount and fight on foot.

[7] In 18 days we covered a distance of 600 versts. (author's note)

[8] Imperial Russian unit of measurement equal to seven feet or 2.13m.

[9] Note. One must also exclude two battalions of the 26th Division, carrying the knapsacks of the two other battalions and not able to arrive for the start of the battle. (author's note)

[10] Paskevich notes in the margins that he had previously engaged in irregular warfare against the Turks.

[11] Barclay de Tolly had detached his I Corps under General Pyotr Wittgenstein, up to 20,000 men, to defend the approaches to St Petersburg.

[12] This section is absent in the second manuscript but present in the first.

[113] Paskevich writes in the margins: "Around 9 o'clock."
[114] Paskevich includes the original French text:

"II (Napoleon) tourna la tacky de I'armee russe, passa Ia Borysthine et se porta sur Smolensk on il arriva 24 heures avant I'armee russe qui refrogarda en toute hute; une division de 15000 russes qui se trouvait standard hasard a Smolensk cut le bonheur de defendre cette place un jour ce qui donna le temps a Barclay de Tolly d'arriver le lendemain. Si I'armee francaise eut surpris Smolensk, elle y eut pas si le Borysthene et attaque standard derriere I'armee russe en desordre et non reunie, ce great upset fut manque."

[115] The text of the second manuscript ends here. The following is taken from the first manuscript.

[116] These were the Maslovo fleches, arrow shaped fortifications near the village of Maslovo. Kutuzov was afraid of being outflanked on the right but in the event these fortifications did not see any action.
[117] This fortification was the famous Grand Redoubt, sometimes referred to as the Raevsky Redoubt as it was manned by the men of General Raevsky's VII Corps.
[118] The three batteries were the famous Semenovskoye or Bagration fleches, after the commander of the Second Army. The fleches witnessed an intense struggle between the two armies and changed hands on several occasions during the battle.
[119] This section appears in the form of Paskevich's pencil notes in the margins of the manuscript.
[120] This section appears in the form of Paskevich's pencil notes in the margins of the manuscript.
[121] A note "NB: 170" appears in the margins. In fact, even this figure vastly overestimates the size of Napoleon's army. The most reliable figures suggest that Napoleon had 130,000 men in the battle and over 500 guns.
[122] This section appears in the form of Paskevich's pencil notes in the margins of the manuscript.
[123] This section appears in the form of Paskevich's pencil notes in the margins of the manuscript.
[124] Paskevich writes "Bonancy."

[25] Wounded heavily and fearing for his life, Bonnamy repeatedly uttered the words 'Je suis le Roi!' He was brought to Kutuzov's headquarters by his captors, who mistakenly thought they had captured Murat, the King of Naples.

[26] Paskevich presumably had Kutaisov in mind. The Russian artillery commander was killed by an enemy artillery shell in the midst of the struggle for the redoubt. Although General Pyotr Konovnitsyn was wounded twice during the battle, he survived and later participated in the famous Council of Fili when Kutuzov made the fateful decision to abandon Moscow.

Printed in Great Britain
by Amazon